Life Beyon

Life Beyond Bullets

A Memoir of Life in Rural Afghanistan
and West Africa

Ankur Mahajan

"Basically, we are all the same human beings with the same potential to be a good human being or a bad human being. The important thing is to realize the positive side and try to increase that; realize the negative side and try to reduce. That's the way."

— Dalai Lama XIV

Disclaimer

The objective of this following memoir is to educate and inform the readers. It is strictly based on the personal experiences of the author and should not be in any way considered as a representation to the author's employer, organization, committee, any Government, group, or individual. The events and conversations in this book have been set down to the best of the author's ability. All accounts are true to the author's knowledge.

The author holds no responsibility on how you'll use the information provided or what you'll do with them. Any content from this book cannot be copied or sold. The reports documented in this memoir are drawn from the experiences of the author, a young man who visited the countries between 2009-2017. The thoughts, opinions, and impressions expressed should not be considered a generalization of the described cultures. They are personal impressions, not meant to disrespect anyone.

Life Beyond Bullets

Memoir of life in rural Afghanistan and West Africa

Copyright © 2021 Ankur Mahajan.

ISBN: 978-1-7773871-3-6 (Paperback)

ISBN: 978-1-7773871-2-9 (Hardcover)

ISBN: 978-1-7773871-1-2 (E-Book)

W: www.lifebeyondbullets.com

E: lifebeyondbullets@gmail.com

Book interior formatting by Abdul Rehman Qureshi

Book cover design by PJCreative

Book edits by Hassan Adesokan

First printing edition 2021.

Dedication

Dedicated to my parents, family, friends, and all children orphaned by war.

I received some of my greatest inspiration and motivation to write this book about ten years ago. It was the day I first visited an orphanage for physically-challenged kids in Uzbekistan. That day, I was so moved that I planned to start a project that would help kids with disabilities in similar circumstances. I later realized that the plight of other kids like them in other war-torn countries was much greater. Nevertheless, they say that the journey of a thousand miles begins with a single step. So, the net royalties of $10,000 from this project will assist NGOs working with these kids.

Acknowledgments

Writing a book about something very important to you can be a surreal process. This publication bears the hands of many, and I appreciate them in no small measures. I am overwhelmed in all humbleness, and pleased to acknowledge my depth of gratitude to all those who have helped me to put these ideas.

Foremost, I give thanks to Lord God Almighty, for protection and perennial guidance. I thank my deceased grandfather, Krishan Lal, and my grandmother, Nirmal Gupta, who showed me the true worth of hard work. Their wise words, encouragement, and an enormous amount of faith in me shaped me into the person I am today.

I am also forever indebted to my parents, Parveen and Rekha Mahajan, who bore me, raised me, supported me, taught me, and loved me unwaveringly. It was under their watchful eye that I gained so much drive and an ability to tackle challenges head-on. Their unflinching courage and conviction have always been an inspiration for me. I equally thank my sisters, Punita and Parul, who have always given me tremendous encouragement and unconditional support through all of these years.

I am immensely thankful to all of my former academic teachers, sports coaches, and other mentors who taught me valuable lessons at various stages throughout my life. My sincere gratitude for their guidance, and for how they instilled confidence and optimism in me. I must thank my first judo teacher Vinod Sharma from Janak Judo Club for pushing me beyond my capacity as a six-year-old with severe asthma.

Some special words of gratitude go to my friends scattered around the world, who have always been a major source of support to me when things get tiring and discouraging. There are so many of them, but I want them to know that I thank each and every one for their thoughts, well-wishes/prayers, phone calls, e-mails, texts, and visits. Particularly helpful to me during this time were Angad, Varun, Nisha and Simran.

Finally, I am extremely grateful to the various organizations and colleagues that I met during global living. To all of the individuals I had the opportunity to lead, to be led by, or to watch their leadership from afar, I say thank you for being the inspiration and foundation for *Life Beyond Bullets*. They all taught me valuable life lessons, and it should go without saying that, without these people, I would not be the person I am today.

Preface

The book addresses the cross-cultural, political, gender, economic, and religious issues of war zones and the least developed nations where I spent many years of my life. My utmost desire is to show the world a picture of these communities with concerns added throughout on ways of fitting in and gaining acceptance and recognition from the resident population.

From the start to the end, I emphasize how people live in these parts of the world and the lifestyle you can expect as a foreigner. Concurrently, I discuss the development ideologies, everyday life, general observations, as well as the dating and marriage culture of these communities. The importance of religion and the complicated issues of health and politics are all documented here, too. I equally highlight the dangers that the locals, several foreigners, and people like myself have faced in a bid to survive in these communities. I also discuss lessons I learned about reintegrating into my own society after returning from various development missions in dangerous and less-developed locales.

Through this book, I hope that my readers will understand the cultural difficulties of immigrants and refugees from places like those

I discuss here, and support them as they arrive in and adapt to more economically developed countries.

Having lived in developing and war-torn countries for many years, I critically dug into my experiences and have shared how life looks in these parts of the world. As you are about to find out, this book goes beyond conventional war and development books that depict the challenges and realities of everyday life, a long distance from the diplomatic and media bubbles most people are familiar with. Hence the title, *Life Beyond Bullets*.

Table of Contents

Chapter 1.

The Background

Curiosity is a strange state of mind that strikes everybody. It is an instinctive urge that sprinkles in your heart and begins to grow in different dimensions. It is something that makes us fall prey to various situations.

Considered an intellectual virtue, it has spurred the greatest inventions and solutions of all time. It depends on who you ask, curiosity has led people to a different point in their lives. The instant you start, you'll find yourself in an absolute inescapable labyrinth. You are bound to have one of two reactions: fear or excitement. How a person reacts, shows just how much of a hold curiosity has over them.

If you recognize curiosity from its earliest spring, you can simply turn around and find security in the everyday activities where little changes and life seems a little greyer.

Entering the labyrinth and choosing to keep going forward into unknown territory can be a difficult choice for some and an inevitability for others. From whatever your starting point, once you commit, you have little choice but to continue into the unknown territory. For those who are accepting, you eventually realize that you're still traversing life's path, but you are taking a path that is more uniquely your own amidst uncertainties.

One noteworthy idealist who completely subscribes to this philosophy is Albert Einstein, having once confessed that, "I have no special talent. I am only passionately curious." These famous words resonated with me, so much so I live by them to this day. But before we begin the journey of how curiosity took me through the wild torrents of life, let me introduce myself.

An Indian guru gave me my name, Ankur, a Hindu name derived from Sanskrit, meaning "a sapling or a blossoming flower." Apparently, he saw peaceful plant-like qualities in me—some sort of strange photosynthesis. This custom of naming is still prevalent in many parts of the world; the third party with no relation to your DNA decides to name you just because your parents or family are devotees. My name did not rhyme with those of my two older siblings. It even started with a different letter, and I wasn't the kind of angelic baby that was peaceful and quiet at all times. So, I would not give the guru an A plus for this job.

Also, I was born on a Tuesday. According to the Hindu calendar, that's the day of Lord Hanuman, the Monkey God. Wielding his golden Gada (a mace), he is a symbol of strength, energy, and courage— an image that doesn't quite align with the "blossoming flower" of my name. The sound of it just did not sound very sexy or masculine, like Rocky Balboa, a name that drops like thunder.

What made it worse, though, was as I was studying French and later lived in France. When pronounced with a French accent, my name sounded close to "un cul," which means "a butt."

Now, I'm sure none of us would like it if some random French boys laughed at your name and called you a butt. *It's not very nice, is it? Neither blossoming flower nor butt were smashing successes, I reckon.*

Later on, though, I learned of an Indian Bollywood movie with the name Ankur. It's a rather famous movie, winning several awards. That was when it struck me that perhaps, the guru who named me had just seen the film, liked it a lot and decided to name me after it. Considering I was born on a Tuesday, and Mondays have cheaper theater and movie tickets, this scenario kind of made sense.

In retrospect, I feel fortunate that he didn't name me after something he'd eaten while watching the movie. "Popcorn" is ten times worse than Ankur.

The mystery behind the reason for this name will probably stay with me to my grave (perhaps the urn, or mountaintop—*who knows what culture I'll be living in when that time comes?*).

As was the case for everyone else, nobody had consulted me at my naming ceremony. Though I'm more than sure, even if they had, I do not think anything would have changed. Had I cried out at the suggestion, they likely would have attributed it to something else and kept the name anyway. It taught me an important lesson, though: either thoroughly research the name you're going to give your child or make sure that guru has good tastes in movies.

When I was almost five years old, I began looking in earnest at the surrounding people, on television, in magazines, and I realized that some had skin colors that differed from mine. I found myself observing people who had skin shades that were pale white, bronze, mocha brown, black, and everything in between- any different skin color was intriguing to me. I also noticed that facial features could be quite different: noses could be flat, protuberant, small, large, narrow, wide, and any combination of the above.

It baffled my young mind, and I began to wonder how children who look so different than me would go about living their lives. Sometimes I'd ask myself different questions:

What types of food do they eat? How do they get along with each other and their families? How much playtime do they have? Do they also get into fights with their siblings?

These questions fascinated me, and my mind latched on to the thought. Sometimes I would get distracted from my studies too. This was the first time where I found myself in a curiosity labyrinth, and it took me down a path that I would never have found without that initial curiosity about people who looked so different from me.

One day, I grew tired of doing all the homework my teacher assigned, and I wondered whether those other kids might also be frustrated with their teachers giving them endless homework. My mind became obsessed with how children from other cultures lived their lives, and I would compare all the things that took up the hours of my days with how they might be living.

Do they also have to perform continuous and unnecessary household chores? Are they forced to visit relatives they don't like? Do their moms also have them attend judo training every day?

At the age of six, something big and round in my classroom caught my eye: my teacher had a globe. This common object did something to my mind that opened up a whole new world – that globe was my Pandora's Box. I looked for my city- *Delhi* and to my absolute shock, what seemed so enormous to me was no more than a tiny speck on that magical globe.

How could this be the case? My jaw dropped in shock.

Spinning the globe on its axis, I read all the lands and oceans as they sped past my astonished eyes. A blur of green and blue. It was the early 1990s (pre-internet), and many important questions swirled through my curious mind. Back then, one could not just ask Alexa for the answers; it would instead take hard work and diligence to get them. You had to go to a library and find encyclopedias or specialized books to get an answer.

I was shocked that my house was not on the globe, and then I realized the even more significant fact that neither my street nor my grandmother's house, which was much larger than my own, was visible before me on the surface of that colorful orb. None of the local street vendors or the crowded streets bustling with people could be seen. Our complete insignificance in relation to the rest of the world frightened and saddened me.

On the globe, I noticed a mass of land that seemed larger than the rest; it was across the ocean. Leaning forward, I saw that the enormous landmass was called Africa.

It was so big that it seemed to encompass a quarter of all the land in the entire world. This realization amazed me and stopped the globe from spinning. I peered closer, squinting to make out the names of the countries and cities spread across its face—places with strange, exotic, and unpronounceable names, like Ouagadougou, Yamoussoukro, or Bolgatanga.

I turned 12 in 1996, imagining it as almost the beginning of my teenage years. It was a time of inner panic for me as my body began to change and betray me, turning me from a child to an adolescent almost overnight.

Yet as my body grew in odd ways, so did my mind. It helped me become more confident in myself. I grew taller, my clothes seemed to shrink, and I began to notice weird changes all over.

Now the biggest curiosity that burned in my mind was the opposite sex: how they looked. More importantly, I began to wonder what I could do with my new form to be more appealing to them. I learned that hormones were the cause of this strange feeling of chaos in my body and loins. They were developing, making my muscles grow, and, strangely, hair sprout all over my body. The boosts of testosterone meant I was running faster and performing better in judo competitions. For the first time, I looked impressive. These changes had one incredibly positive effect – my siblings were far less likely to pick fights with me.

It all happened so quickly that my excitement blended with fear.

How different would I be once this transformation had ended?

Everything felt strange, and suddenly all I wanted to do was hang out with different people at school; I wanted to be a very popular kid. Life wasn't keeping up with the pace of my mental changes—*I craved new adventures; I felt restless.*

My old interest in new places grew into a deep curiosity. I badly wanted to see these foreign lands, and I was hungry to visit most if not all of them. This urge to explore lingered in my thoughts, always nudging and yanking at the back of my mind.

It wasn't long after that when I saw the news about the Taliban taking over Afghanistan. Those rustic-looking men captivated me with their scraggly beards, strange clothes, and big guns, always shouting *Allahu Akbar!* (God is most great) I had no idea what they were celebrating, but they always seemed to be shouting. I looked closer at the fragmented images of Afghanistan's soiled streets, where women wore blue burqas. I had nothing other than school uniforms to compare with these images. So, I reasoned, that's what they must be. It made me content to imagine that our school uniforms were so much better.

Those quirky TV images further fueled my interests and imagination. I had to learn more about Afghanistan. In those pre-Google days, I relied on an enormous set of encyclopedias that my mother had bought years prior. I flipped through the pages filled with small print and bright illustrations. At last, I found "Afghanistan."

However, to my disappointment, the entry said this mysterious country was in the middle of a war.

I sighed, and a sense of sorrow washed over me. War was a word I knew very well. All Indian children did. We learned at a young age that we were perpetually at war with Pakistan and that someday we would be called upon to fight them, and not just in cricket. In simpler and shorter words, they are our enemies—enemies that we had not met, but were supposed to hate nonetheless.

Who would know that, years later, I would be living with Pakistanis and consider them some of my best friends?

At that moment, I filed Afghanistan away, at least temporarily, as akin to Pakistan and synonymous with a looming battle that I would have no choice but to fight.

As I grew older and started high school, my teachers told us about the history of Afghanistan, how the Soviet Union had invaded that country, and that the USA was the hero. They were fighting the Taliban, which I now learned was a terrorist group that took over the country and were ruthlessly ruling it with barbaric ways. The years passed by, and we continued hearing about the Taliban. Their long beards and that super serious and repulsive look on their faces appalled me. They were so scary and distasteful to many of us that we started to refer to some of our least-favorite teachers as Taliban.

Of course, I was completely misguided about that, as those teachers were just doing their best to improve the futures of us mischievous and obnoxious teenagers, while the Taliban were ruining thousands of lives who were unfortunate to stand in their way to power and control.

I further imagined that I would never be close to those inhumane, filthy-looking people—*Who would want to be?*

Unfortunately, the best-laid plans, the most honest intentions, everything that we want to believe about ourselves when we are children and teens can get warped, and that happened to me.

Well, I was wrong about that too, as you will see.

When I was in high school in 2001, the Twin Towers in New York City were destroyed in a plume of dust and debris, and several thousand people died. This was very painful to all of my family and friends, as we witnessed those innocent lives lost in smoke, flames, and steel in what seemed like just a few minutes. It seemed impossible that the day could start so innocently, then in a matter of hours, everything could be turned upside-down.

Then we heard the word Taliban literally every hour on the news. They were officially the worst villains of the world, and I gained a feeling of reassurance when we heard that the hero (the United States) was fighting the evil Taliban to save us all.

That anger and sadness quickly gave way to the everyday reality of my teenage life. Life continued with academics, extracurricular activities, sports, music, chatting on ICQ/MSN, and other mundane teenage issues, which at the time looked as if the world depended on them. The movie Titanic had made its debut in 1998 with the perfect love mania that would be in vogue for decades—us kids were on deck. I still remember how girls in my class would blush at the mere picture of Leonardo di Caprio. For the boys, we were more concerned about how lucky he was to have won a tight spot beside Kate Winslet. While everyone else was swooning over the movies, current events resonated with me in a much deeper way, in print, and on screens.

Luckily, as much as the mundanities of life had kept me occupied, I would soon get to explore a world beyond what I knew: in my late teen years, I moved out of my parents' house.

That curiosity of seeing Africa had never left me. However, I remembered my family's strong emphasis on a good education. So, I had already traveled to many countries, but those trips were all student exchange programs or internships in other developed nations of Europe and Oceania. I was so accustomed to the North American, Australian, and European cultures that I started considering all the material comfort people enjoyed there not as a want but as a need. I was well settled and comfortable in my ways and hobbies that world economics and international news did not bother me as much as they once did.

In 2008, I turned 24, and I completed my first master's degree. With such an achievement, I began looking around for other opportunities to explore. That's when I came across an organization called AIESEC (a French acronym for Association Internationale des étudiants en sciences économiques et commerciales), but now officially known by the acronym. It is a student organization that finds internships for people in various countries. I thought an international internship would be a splendid opportunity for me since; I was still young and wanted to see more of the world. Sold on the idea, I promptly registered for membership to see where the organization would take me.

They sent me a form to list my preferences of countries for their first development trainee internship, and I completed the form stating that I had no preference for any country. I was willing to go anywhere.

This was easy for me to say at the time because I had no loans to repay – my parents covered all of the expenses for my academic studies. Without a financial limitation, I was open to opportunities that weren't necessarily financially lucrative.

When AIESEC responded with an opportunity, I enthused on the phone with them, letting them know that I was still open to wherever the internship was. They told me that I was going to a location where the people spoke French, but the name of the country that they said was garbled. They ended the call and simply said that I could consider my choice, then let them know once I had reached a decision. I couldn't quite make out the place, but it started with "Cote," so I figured it must be some small place that would really give me a unique experience.

Intrigued, I googled places starting with "Cote" that spoke French, and the very first search led me to "Côte d'Azur." I saw pictures of a beautiful place with exotic beaches that made my heart race with excitement. I felt blessed to have the opportunity to go to such a beautiful location. To start, my experience on the Mediterranean coast of southeastern France was perfect. In a heartbeat, I'd canceled or withdrawn all of my other applications.

The next day, I called them and told them just how willing I was to take the internship. I informed them I was ready to come as soon as possible, and they should start preparing my paperwork. It was still summer, so I would need to be patient about finally seeing those beautiful beaches of the Côte d'Azur where I could swim and run during my days off.

My excitement overwhelmed every other emotion. Soon came the email with an attachment for my visa and insurance paperwork—I'd never felt this glad to fill out the paperwork!

As I printed the document to read it, gnawing on my lip in anticipation, my eyes scanned over the paragraphs. Suddenly, the exhilaration that had built up inside of me popped clean through my chest, leaving me feeling hollow. My skin tingled, and my throat felt tight as the truth finally emerged.

The location was not Côte d'Azur, but rather Côte d'Ivoire, in Africa.

Okay—clearly, I'd made an error. I quickly shook my head, thinking that this would probably be a perfectly acceptable substitute. Willing myself back into a state of excitement, I focused on reviewing everything I had to look forward to during my internship.

Things did not improve. As I read through the documents, I saw that there was a long list of vaccines that would be required to get to enter Côte d'Ivoire. At this stage, I knew absolutely nothing about the country as that was the first time I had even heard the nation's name.

A sense of dread gnawed at me, and I decided to research a little before going any further. After typing Côte d'Ivoire into my computer, I began to feel a cold sweat as the images that appeared were nothing like the inviting beaches that had been the highlight of my anticipation. Instead, I saw huge African men holding heavy guns that looked terrifying.

I felt the sweat trickle down my neck as I saw the pictures. *What had this "blossoming flower" gotten himself into?*

With trepidation, I began looking over the news about the country, and it was mostly about the casualties of political riots or other conflicts. Here I had been planning on sunbathing on the French Riviera while listening to Edith Piaf and eating freshly baked croissants every day. Instead, my internship would be in a war zone. I had to accept swimming in the ocean, and the balmy French summer was a fleeting fantasy now.

Sitting down at my desk, I quietly contemplated the future. I pictured myself standing in a desolate place, witnessing the violence of the utmost extreme. Years of having judo training wouldn't provide me much of an edge against automatic rifles.

Despite all of my concern and panic, I decided not to reject the internship straight away—I wanted to think about it now that I had more details, to consider if this was actually something that would really push the boundaries of my understanding of the world. This decision would prove to be fundamental to me for almost the next eight years as it would wrench me out of my complacency and throw me into a world that I hadn't really thought about in years. Looking back, I feel so lucky to have made that decision.

The next morning, I was still recovering from the confusion of Côte d'Azur and Côte d'Ivoire. I forced my mind to consider my new reality, my real internship in a place that I wasn't mentally prepared to visit. Flipping on the TV, I was drawn to the news, which as a young adult I found more interesting, almost like a surrogate to my interest in the world when I was young, but with a lot more understanding of what I was learning. What greeted me was the story about an Air France flight that had crashed into the Atlantic Ocean, off the coast of Brazil, on a flight from Rio de Janeiro to Paris. All 228 passengers and crew of this flight died. As I stared in shock at the timing of such a tragic story, I couldn't help but feel it was a reminder that there are no guarantees in life, no matter where you are in the world. There are inherent risks to being alive that are true whether you are in a developing country or a developed one. No matter where I go, I'm always at risk for death.

I was still in my early twenties and willing to live in other countries. If I was to ever work in a conflict zone, this was the time to learn more about myself and my own abilities in adversity. After some serious contemplation of weighing the pros and cons of what going through with the internship would mean in my life, I decided to honor my acceptance of the internship. After all, I had a failsafe that wasn't available to the people who live there; if at any moment I felt threatened, I could just leave the country.

Even though I'd made my decision, convincing my parents was much harder—even for my mother, who always pushed me to take chances. I promised them that if I ever felt threatened or uncomfortable with any situation regarding safety, I would come back as soon as possible. It took a lot of work, but they eventually agreed that I could go, though the hesitation and uncertainty were evident in their voices and expressions. In retrospect, I don't know how I managed to overcome their reluctance – pure luck is probably the best explanation.

The initial shock turned into a different kind of excitement. Those early 10-year-old dreams of seeing the large, colorful continent on the globe were about to come true. Even better, I was not going as a tourist or even as a student, but as an intern who would be working in an active conflict zone. Perhaps it wasn't quite what I had imagined, but it would undoubtedly provide a much more unique understanding.

And isn't that what we really want? A more realistic understanding of the world around us.

This was my chance to really learn about a small part of the continent. I knew that it wasn't a representation of the entire continent – the size of the place had been what had initially impressed me – but it was a start. I was finally back in that curiosity labyrinth. My apprehension shifted to enthusiasm, so by the time I boarded the plane, I had no doubts that my world was about to change.

And it was, though not in the way I had thought. I will never forget those first few weeks in Côte d'Ivoire – the sights, the sounds, the smells were all unlike anything I had ever experienced. The people were hospitable; there were beautiful, undulating hills and even beaches. What actually took me by surprise was that the people were fundamentally similar to myself and those I loved.

Those questions that had plagued my imagination when I was young now seemed to be answered – *those children probably did feel the same way that I had.* The realization that we had a lot in common helped me to realize that exploring the world holds an inexhaustible wealth of things to learn.

By the time I had finished my brief time as an intern, I felt that I had been successful in handling the responsibilities of working in a conflict zone. The experience opened my eyes to the astounding strength and kindness of the country's residents and the kinds of challenges that developing nations faced. Out of this internship, I developed a sense of purpose. I had a strong desire to give back to humanity because I had a better understanding of just what some people experienced. I was inspired to work in similar places around the globe.

Since then, I have worked in Uzbekistan and China, and the rural areas of Ghana and Afghanistan. Deciding to go to these places required courage, especially the war-torn Afghanistan. It is a country that is constantly in the news, but rarely for a good reason. Often invaded over the centuries, but mostly never defeated. The country was now the scene of frequent abductions, almost daily suicide bombings, and operations by major-power intelligence agencies—the CIA (USA), SVR (successor to the KGB's foreign office), RAW (India), ISI (Pakistan), and so many others lost to history. The keenness and enthusiasm to help the people had gotten the better of my caution, and so I went.

For the next ten years, I celebrated my birthday in a new different country every year – and that was how I spent my 20s. From that one miscommunication about my internship, I started down a path that I could never have foreseen. Looking back at my life, I am extremely glad that things unfolded as they did.

Chapter 2.

Daily Life and Cultural Observations

Since the very start of humanity, wars and conflicts have been a significant portion of our history. People worldwide, regardless of their race, have been involved in many kinds of battles, fought over everything from personal to religious causes.

Some of those conflicts were over in days, and some were fought for several, or even many, generations. Afghanistan, a mountainous country in Central Asia, is not a stranger to this gruesome misery. Its present war caused tremendous damage to the country, not only economically but also culturally, and its effects have spilled into the neighboring countries of Tajikistan and Uzbekistan as well. Another country that has been sorely affected by the Afghan war is Pakistan due to its similar culture, its closeness with the Afghan people, and the active role that Pakistanis have played in the Afghan war.

Similarly, African countries have suffered long from ruthless and corrupt political leaders. These individuals were either elected by non-transparent "democratic" processes or through elections rigged by more powerful nations. One such country is Côte d'Ivoire, also known as Ivory Coast, with its Atlantic coastline and bordering countries of Liberia, Ghana, Guinea, Mali, and Burkina Faso. It has a long history of political turbulence and civil conflict. Sadly, the beautiful country of Côte d'Ivoire is known to most people for its civil wars and unrest.

But to get back to Afghanistan's basics, it is landlocked and mountainous, surrounded by Pakistan, Iran, Turkmenistan, Uzbekistan, Tajikistan, and just a bit of far western China. The country contains most of the Hindu Kush mountain range. It is those high mountains that, even though they might have hindered the unity of Afghanistan, have protected the country from numerous foreign attacks over the centuries; neither the British nor the Soviets were able to conquer the land.

This is the land where great world powers have fought: Alexander the Great, Arab Muslims, the Mongols under Genghis Khan, the British, Soviets, and Americans have all fought on this land.

Afghan culture reflects the historical events and conflicts that have shaped the behavior of the people. From what I have seen, these conflicts have influenced the people to lead a more conservative life, one in which they are less likely to trust outsiders and strangers. This also created a dominant religious society; as the people dealt with daily uncertainties, their faith in God only grew.

In my experience, the presence of foreigners in the country, be it for development or security, reminds the locals of their colonial past and how outside powers tried to extract their natural resources. In general, the same result has occurred in other developing and war-torn countries with a history of powerful nations invading them.

When I was in Côte d'Ivoire and Ghana, people would sometimes act distant to me, or I might hear a stray comment based solely on a person's race. I learned that many Africans in rural areas identify only three races: African, Chinese (often all Asians are perceived as being Chinese due to the pervasiveness of China in the media), and Caucasian. So, you could be of Arabian or Indian descent but would still be considered white, and hence, you would be the target of racist remarks meant for North Americans or Europeans.

Personal Attire

When it comes to personal attire, in bigger cities such as Abidjan in Côte d'Ivoire or Accra in Ghana, many people dress in Western clothing. Women and men alike wear shorts and other types of garments common in big cities everywhere.

In Afghanistan, however, men and women are strictly prohibited from wearing shorts or sleeveless shirts in public, though Kabul is much more liberal in this regard than rural areas and smaller cities. Still, the culture tends to be very conservative. In Afghan cities such as Kandahar or Fayzabad, you could attract stares and angry looks if you dress more liberally.

To feel more a part of the culture in Afghanistan, I have found that a regular *salwar kameez* (traditional clothing for men and women) generally works. It is highly accepted and creates greater credibility when dealing with the locals. Even while jogging or playing soccer, Afghan men seldom wear shorts; it is usually the salwar kameez for all occasions.

On the other hand, in Ghana and Côte d'Ivoire, wearing trousers is very typical, and wearing a shirt with an African print will usually attract compliments from the locals. People of all cultures appreciate foreigners' attempts to fit in. Most see it as a sign of respect for their traditions and lifestyle.

Like the traditional dress, facial hair has a special significance in Afghanistan. I found that having a beard helped me in several ways. For instance, many Afghans did not notice me as a foreigner until I spoke due to my facial features and skin tone. So, during field visits, I was always perceived to be a local. I believe this kept me safe and reduced the natural suspicion of local villagers and other people I met during my field visits. While walking the streets of Kabul, I never noticed any stares, which I believe had a lot to do with my dressing like a local.

During the field visits, I observed that people thought I was an Afghan due to my skin tone and my preference for their traditional attire. But the instant they realized that I was a foreigner, they became very nice to me. They were more excited to learn that I am of Indian origin. It was not different in Ghana and Côte d'Ivoire, where many would even stop to take selfie pictures with me. The children loved to shake hands with me, and some would stop to wave, saying, "welcome to Ghana".

In this aspect, western African communities are much more easy-going. Of course, this depends somewhat on regional mores, but this part of the world is generally much more accepting. You can be yourself if you do not dress inappropriately or vulgarly and stand out.

In the countries where I worked, I often experienced shortages of office equipment and supplies. It seemed like only big private companies and international organizations had sufficient supplies; smaller NGOs and companies almost always struggled. New startups and small NGOs must make do with fewer resources. Sometimes I had to share my work computer with another person or two. This often led to less job satisfaction, and so many workers are not able to be as productive as they would have been if they had sufficient resources.

There is also a major shortage of public toilets in most of the developing world and conflict areas. In cities in Western Africa and Afghanistan, public urination by men is considered extremely impolite. Of course, this happens very often, but if you are caught in the act, you might quickly find yourself in an ugly or even violent situation. I have even heard of people in Ghana being killed after being caught in the act of urination on someone else's property.

Greetings and Physical Contact

Each culture has its own distinct ways of greeting to signify recognition, affection, friendship, and reverence. Even so, shaking hands is generally a promising approach in most countries. In Afghanistan, people always begin conversations with *assalam alaykum* (peace be upon you), the most common greeting, and then proceed to ask about each other's wellbeing and each other's family. Even professional emails always start with the standard greetings and then move on to the presently relevant issues. Asking about the wellbeing of someone's family and passing greetings to members of another's family is always a polite and appreciated gesture.

In West Africa, owing to the French influence there, you will also see people kissing each other's cheeks as a greeting, especially if at least one of them is a foreigner. However, among the locals, it is generally a handshake between individuals of the same sex, or sometimes it is just a "hello." Cheek kissing between opposite sexes is common and acceptable in Côte d'Ivoire, depending on the region.

In Afghanistan, men shake hands and sometimes hug or kiss each other's cheeks if they know each other well. Individuals of the opposite gender do not touch each other while greeting unless they are direct family members. Some unexpected paradoxes of greeting in Afghanistan include Afghan men's comfort in shaking hands with foreign women, but Afghan women will not or will very seldom shake hands with foreign men. In my experience, Afghan women never shake hands with the opposite sex in a gathering with other Afghan men. During seminars and field missions near the Afghanistan-Tajikistan border, I saw that Afghan men would shake hands with

Tajik women during our meetings, but when greeting Afghan women, they would instead place a hand on their heart as a gesture of respect.

If you are a foreign man visiting Afghanistan, you should always maintain a distance between yourself and Afghan women. Afghan men watch the behaviors of foreign men around local women closely, especially initially. They equally keep a close watch when the foreign man is youthful and single.

In Ghana and Côte d'Ivoire, however, things are different. There, the office culture is very much as it is in North America, where men and women observe pretty much the same modes of greeting. Foreign men and women do not attract any untoward attention if they eat with local colleagues of the opposite gender.

It is interesting to note that many Afghans and Africans respect and use their right hands a lot more than their left. They shake hands, eat, hand objects to people, and so on with their right hands. They practically assumed the left hand is offensive, unclean and should not be used the same way as the right. They often reject handshakes or objects handed to them with the left hand. They believe the left hand is used for "ablution." So, you should remember any time you are in one of these countries, use your right hands to relate with people.

Dining & Household Customs

When it comes to food, most West African cuisines are spicy compared to that of Afghanistan, though in both cases, meat is usually the center of the meal. The concepts of vegetarian, vegan, or gluten-free diets are almost unknown. As food is always in short supply in most conflict areas, people sometimes eat the same kind of staple meal every day. Food diversity can therefore be extremely low unless one is a diplomat or earns a high income. Then supermarkets with imports would cater to one's diet.

In most developing nations, people generally prefer heavier breakfasts. This meal is almost always savory in Afghanistan and Ghana, but in Côte d'Ivoire, some people have French cakes and croissants for breakfast due to France's history there. Students usually have coffee and a baguette with butter or sometimes porridge.

It is interesting to see the heavy legacy of colonialism on cuisines. People in Ghana are more inclined to drink tea due to British influence, while neighboring Côte d'Ivoire and Burkina Faso have more coffee drinkers. Also, Ghanaians prefer a British style loaf of bread, while Ivorians and Burkinabe are more likely to eat French baguettes.

The manner of eating in areas of Central Asia like Tajikistan, Uzbekistan, and Afghanistan is entirely different from the developed world. People sit and have a meal on a rug on the floor. Cross-legged, they sit in parallel towards each other with food and cutleries set in between them, and their backs facing the wall. I consider this comfortable and frugal since no furniture expenses are incurred. Only a few homes consider the need for cushions, which remain inexpensive compared to proper chairs. It is rude to step on the rug or pass the spot where the food is served. It is equally wrong to walk in-between the people having a meal. One can only walk behind anyone sitting. Generally, men and women eat separately except for close families, and in some households, women are not permitted to eat before their husbands.

In Afghan and African cultures alike, people tend to use their hands more than cutlery when eating, especially in Ghana, where people eat even hot curries and soups without cutlery, using bread or dough as a spoon.

In Afghanistan, the food is very similar to that of Uzbekistan and Tajikistan; in many places, people even eat kebabs for breakfast. There is not much variation among the three daily meals, but for breakfast, some will have eggs and *shir chai* (a salty Afghan tea with walnuts).

Every developing country experiences a scarcity of primary resources that few in Europe or America can imagine. Afghans and West Africans save precious little food or water, and they recycle their clothes and other material possessions more often than folks in the Western countries. Material things have much more value and stay in use longer. Parents and grandparents often yell at younger children for wasting food and water.

Most children have few, if any, fancy toys, and when they do, the precious items usually come recycled from older siblings, cousins, or even neighbors. The same goes for fancy clothes, which family and friends share and borrow. This ethic of community sharing benefits all, and most everyone realizes it.

If you have never been to a low-income country before, the evidence of poverty can overwhelm you. I remember that Ivoirians often would use kola nuts to kill their hunger when they did not have the means to obtain food. These nuts have high caffeine content and can help to ease hunger. They are cheap and so many use them when they are traveling or would like to save money for food. It was very disheartening to see that, especially when I was aware of the massive amounts of food that people in high-income countries waste every day.

I was interested to see that, in West Africa, many people eat the bones and feet of their chickens. They also use chicken fat in many of their dishes, and that's just chickens. Literally, every animal in sub-Saharan Africa that can be easily caught is used for food, from dogs to monkeys.

Some restaurants in villages serve a dish called "bush meat," which is the meat of wild animals, though it most often refers to the remains of animals killed in the forests and savannas of Africa. There are several different kinds of bush meats, including long hunted bats, monkeys, rats, snakes, and other wild animals used for sustenance.

In villages, little shops provide only the very basic necessities; I often saw food for sale long past its "best if used by" date. In such places, you should always use plenty of caution when consuming milk- and meat-based products. To be on the safe side, have them only if they are served hot.

Besides that, I also noticed that green tea is the most common beverage in Central Asia. This might owe to their cold weather conditions. On the flip side, West African communities like Ghana and Côte d'Ivoire barely take hot drinks; their temperature is milder than what is observed in Central Asia.

In Western Africa, most people dip their hands in a small bowl of water to wash them before eating. Almost all restaurants in Côte d'Ivoire and Ghana, even the smaller ones, have such facilities. Individuals pass the same bowl of water to each other but rarely change the water. Consequently, after six or seven, people have used the water, it is incredibly filthy. This is one of the easiest ways to pass infections unknowingly from one person to another, especially since eating with one's hands is the cultural norm.

When it comes to Afghanistan's languages, Dari and Pashto are the official and most widely spoken ones. The south of the country speaks mostly Pashto (and/or Urdu, due to the long border with Pakistan). The north inhabitants mostly speak Dari, but many also understand a bit of Russian because of the borders there with former

Soviet republics. In Kabul, most international organizations usually use English, but in rural areas, they use the local languages; if some workers for the organizations have difficulty with the local languages, they will have translators for them.

I found it interesting to learn that Dari is an Afghan dialect of Persian and that inhabitants of Tajikistan and Iran also speak it. In both Afghanistan and Iran, it's written in Arabic characters, so a lot of books in Afghanistan come from Iran. In Tajikistan, however, Dari is written in Cyrillic characters. So interestingly, Tajiks can speak to Afghans, but they cannot read Dari books in Afghanistan, and Afghans cannot read Cyrillic. Contrary in Pakistan, Urdu is written with Arabic characters, just like Dari in Afghanistan, so Pakistanis can read Dari in Afghanistan but cannot fully understand what it means.

In Ghana, Côte d'Ivoire, and most of sub-Saharan Africa generally, there are about 50 to 80 indigenous languages, and they can change drastically from one village to another. Naturally, this also creates barriers, causes ethnic discrimination, and ultimately disrupts the harmony of these countries.

Context of Respect

The cultures of most low-income countries accord special respect to older relatives and figures of authority. In the home, one always addresses others with an honorific such as uncle, aunt, sister, and brother, even if the people involved are not closely related. In public settings in Afghanistan, women are not addressed or referred to by their names. This custom extends even to wedding invitations and tombstones, which identify women in terms of being the daughter, wife, or mother of (a named) father, husband, or eldest son. Many Afghans believe that the public utterance of a woman's name dishonors her.

Afghans also have a special way of referring to their friends and colleagues. Instead of merely calling each other by their names, they append the suffix *-ji* or *-jan* to the name. In other words, colleagues with the names of Abdul and Bahara will refer to each other as Abduljan or Baharaji. The custom of adding -ji comes from India and Pakistan, while the custom of adding -jan comes from Central Asia. These are gestures of respect and warmth towards the other person. In work situations, one always addresses one's superior *sahib* (male) or *sahiba* (female). And one also always uses an individual's occupational title when addressing them. For instance, if your boss had the name Rahman, you would refer to him as "Engineer Rahman sahib." One refers to one's friends and domestic help such as cleaners, cooks, or security guards with the title *aka*, which means brother. So if you have a friend named Gul, you would refer to him as "Aka Gul."

In public situations in Ghana and Côte d'Ivoire, good manners dictate that you refer to elderly women as *mama* or *sister*; for elderly men, the titles are *master* or *sir*. When speaking to or about their superiors, workers never use the individuals' given names. In more familiar settings, such as among friends of similar age and outside of a professional environment, people call each other *chale*, which is roughly equivalent to the American *dude*.

These cultures emphasize respect in personal greetings. Even at work, every conversation begins by greeting the other person with a "good morning" or "good afternoon." Then come the inquiries about each other's health and how the other's family is doing. The notion of respectful references is very well incorporated into Asian and African cultures, and so referring to people older or at a senior rank to you without a respectful title can be considered rude.

In Ghana, I was called "Master" by the schoolboys. While it might sound of racist origin, the word has no racist connotation to them.

They are trained to address their male teachers as "Master" and the females as "Mummy" or "Mistress." A young unmarried female teacher is considered a "Mistress," and a married female teacher is "Mummy." Master is also sometimes used to address elderly men as a sign of respect.

Another factor of many African and Asian cultures to keep in mind is that parents and teachers discipline children through fear of punishment more than through shaming. In China, Afghanistan, and African countries, physical punishment by child-authority figures is very prevalent, and this sometimes results in physical harm. Jokes tend to be more physical, and culturally you just have less physical space in these places than you do in high-income countries.

I would never advocate physical punishment in schools or at home, but I can say this: students tend to be much more respectful and obedient in Asian and African countries than what I have seen here in North America. In those cultures, children learn to respect their elders and teachers at an early age, whereas in the West, respect does not come automatically with age.

In all low-income and strife-torn countries, greeting others properly and showing concern for their wellbeing is a very vital aspect in developing a trusting relationship. People always value expressions of empathy. Things are not as they are in high-income countries, where people tend to dispense with formalities and cut straight to the issue at hand. I have found that expressing empathy in standard everyday greetings goes a long way toward developing relationships based on trust. You will find that your colleagues and employees will be motivated to add more value to the work they do. They will, in turn, find you more approachable and be more willing to share their work ideas and issues with you.

It is ideal to remain formal when serving in western countries or head offices with other international staff. It is a strict setting. So, there are no responsibilities beyond the direct tasks assigned to each person. This makes it easy for most international staff in such places to adopt the "brief-and-be-gone" strategy. In essence, they can be brief and gone with no complications. But this is not the case for anyone who works with people directly in rural areas.

One cannot be successful by staying aloof to the people around them. It is necessary to express concern for the people and their families' wellbeing. One should be approachable, interesting, and respectful. One needs to be empathetic too. The residents often express their pains, hardship, and their deep thoughts to people who appear to share their distress. They also appreciate people who have a sense of humor. They like to see that one can crack and take jokes without getting offended. Spending enough time with them is an exciting way to learn their language. It also proves to be way more interesting than attending diplomatic parties organized by embassies and foreign staff.

Essentially, each international staff must bear in mind that rural residents revere their culture and religion. They do not tolerate disrespect to these domains, whether it was intended or a joke.

I have seen situations in Afghanistan and Ghana in which bosses from high-income countries showed absolutely no or very little interest in the lives or culture of their in-country peers and subordinates. Unsurprisingly, they received virtually no respect if they were out of sight.

Many international professionals come to low-income countries with a feeling of superiority and fail to show any interest in the local culture. Having an excellent background in development issues will do you no good if you fail to connect with local people on a level of personal trust. You will never have their full commitment to your program. Even if you belong to a different religion, you should learn about the religious context of the country where you are stationed.

Examples of cultural and religious terminology in Afghanistan, that you should understand include Mahram policy, Islamic marital jurisprudence, Islamic sexual jurisprudence and so on; knowing them would prove to be incredibly beneficial when trying to connect with people and formulate policies accordingly.

Another aid in connecting with local co-workers is having hobbies in common. For Afghans and Ghanaians, this could be football, cricket, or music. Sharing leisure interests facilitates not only casual conversations but also enjoying those activities with your staff, which strengthens team unity. Most of the people in low-income countries are very social and have a boundless curiosity about Western and outside cultures, so interacting with them on various topics of conversation makes them feel more comfortable and gives you the opportunity to learn about their culture and general perspectives.

Throughout Central Asia and sub-Saharan Africa, people have the custom, while having lunch or a snack, to share their food with you. Some people from high-income countries, where eating is often a private matter, find this strange. During my time in those countries, I learned how rude it is if you fail to politely offer some of your food to others, even just as a gesture. People of every economic class will always offer you to join them as they eat their food. In Ghana, the most common phrase in offering a bit of one's food is "Please, you are invited." You will hear those words very often.

Another prevalent custom in low-income countries is that whenever colleagues go out together for a meal with the head of the organization, the boss pays for everyone. Among friends, the usual scenario is for someone to pay for all; friends take turns in being the host, so to speak. You will seldom "go Dutch," when each person pays for him- or herself unless the group of friends is unusually large. Celebrating birthdays is another tradition that is topsy-turvy compared to that in high-income countries. Usually, the person who is having a birthday celebration will pay for others if the group dines at a restaurant. So, if you're celebrating a birthday in a low-income country, don't expect to be treated to your meal. Rather, it is expected that you treat others on your birthday.

Children in a Patriarchal Society

In much of the developing world, most families have three or four children, as more children are seen as an assurance of security for the future. Having more children can also be a sign of a man's strength and vitality as well. Further, higher infant mortality rates typically lead many people to have more children than they would have had if better healthcare was available. If someone in either Afghanistan or West Africa leaves behind a large family with many grandchildren, the culture sees this as positive and respectable.

These countries, and most low-GDP and conflict-torn countries, have no social security systems. As such one's family is usually one's most significant asset. Males are the guardians and have a strong responsibility to protect their female relatives. Males also run all errands that require outside interactions.

Since there are no hopes or social security from the government, the family's support is the most valuable asset everyone has. Parents actively play parts in the upbringing of their children. Children, in turn, grow to love, respect, and appreciate their parents. Even when he is married, the first son typically brings the parents into his home and sees to their welfare. People even name their businesses after their parents out of love and respect. This is prevalent in both Asian and African communities. It is unlike Western society where a young person is deemed irresponsible if they continue to live with their parents after a certain age.

Hospitality

In general, Afghans and Ghanaians tend to be very hospitable. Your local colleagues will often invite you to their houses for feasts. People can be amiable and hospitable to foreigners and expatriates. In Afghanistan, when foreigners are a family's only guests, sometimes they will introduce you to their female family members. Within the Afghan community generally, however, girls and women do not eat with male guests unless the guests are very close family members.

Throughout my time spent in Western Africa and Afghanistan, most of the people I interacted with showed great hospitality towards foreigners. Most African and Asian cultures have a proverb to the effect of "Guests should be treated like God." People in those cultures raise their children to believe that the sharing of food and belongings with others is a noble gesture. I have witnessed this behavior many times when, as a guest, I have been repeatedly encouraged to eat my fill.

Children also learn that, if they are guests in someone's house, they should act with more reserve and accept food only reluctantly even if they are hungry; hosts recognize this as a sign of a good upbringing and appropriate modesty. For their part, good hosts typically insist that guests eat their share and more of what is available. Your host may place food on your plate and kindly tell you to eat it all. Such hospitality can be overwhelming, especially when you are the guest of an economically deprived family. The best thing to do in such instances is simply to enjoy the food visibly; this will gratify your hosts and give you your most memorable Asian/African hospitality experience.

There are rules governing hospitality within the Afghan home. In Afghanistan, it is customary to remove your shoes before entering a home. The houses I visited were clean, and they often have slippers at the entrance for their guests to wear around the house. The slippers worn inside are never worn outside, and vice versa.

In my interactions, Africans tend to laugh and smile more than Europeans or North Americans. Practically every Ghanaian and Ivorian I met had a relaxed attitude and an inquisitiveness about foreign cultures. People always greet foreigners when they see them on the streets of Accra and Abidjan. Many even want to shake hands or have their picture taken with you, so this custom makes making friends easy.

Of course, every culture appreciates foreigners who speak the local language; even just a greeting in the local language of a village will ease your relationship with the locals. All Afghans, Uzbeks, Tajiks, and Africans tend to be curious about other nationalities and their ways of living. But in North America, people usually begin asking personal questions only after they have known you for a bit.

The curiosity and friendliness that you can find in almost every part of the low-income countries are due in part to the local population's belief that your presence in their land came about through your altruism and that of the development organization or NGO that sponsored/employed you. Many people have also started realizing that the presence of foreign tourists in their country helps to boost their livelihoods. It augments the revenue generated through tourism. As such, they usually treat foreigners with respect and courtesy.

On the other hand, some local populations in high-income countries can perceive the presence of immigrants as being there to utilize their resources.

In my opinion, it is the media that also plays a significant part and gives an impression of immigrants as having had a difficult past, and that life in other parts of the world is much more challenging. However, that may not be true in every case, as many in developing nations enjoy a high standard of living, and immigrate for various reasons.

Early Education

In Côte d'Ivoire, I volunteered to teach English and math to the neighborhood kids in the evenings. I was amazed by their enthusiasm for learning. It was incredible. My students ranged from five to twelve years old, and I could tell from my experience teaching in other countries that these young African students were much more disciplined than I had expected.

After a few months, I began to realize that educational progress here faced its most substantial obstacle, not in the desire of students to learn, but rather the lack of educational opportunities and family pressure to drop out of school to either care for younger siblings or assume other household responsibilities. So, younger children had more enthusiasm for learning than their older siblings, who tend to lose their passion for learning as the struggles of daily life take their toll.

While I was teaching students, I observed that the system of education emphasizes memorization rather than comprehension. It demands students remember the definitions rather than critically think and understand the concepts.

Most exams have questions that are based on writing rather than an application or multiple-choice questions. Eventually, such a learning style reflects on the ability of the students to perform professionally. They have memorized the concepts, but they are unable to adjust their mindset and apply the contexts in their professions. While this style of teaching appears to not encourage internalization and application of lessons, there are a few positive sides. For instance, schools often stop their students from using calculators. This means the students have to manually calculate and, in the process, sharpen their math skills. It explains why students in these communities are better at math compared to North American students on average.

Another facet of education in Africa is that families have an average of 3-4 children, plus their extended families. It is common for parents to send their kids to live with family members who have better access to schools. Therefore, the oldest child in the household is given responsibility for all of their younger siblings and cousins, and taking care of them can impact the oldest child's growth as well. This additional responsibility is known to impact their concentration in school.

Another stumbling-block to educational progress is the lack of educated role models in African neighborhoods. If children have no models of well-educated and successful people to emulate, they lack that deep incentive to continue their own educations. Unfortunately, many Ivoirians who did receive a good education and went on to a successful career leave Côte d'Ivoire for France or other foreign lands.

On the rare occasions that they return home, their neighbors and family enthusiastically welcome and look up to them. So the children would grow up witnessing the respect that educated and successful Ivorian's living abroad can command. As it is, however, these visits back home only fuel the perception that life anywhere else is better, and so the brain drain only accelerates.

Of course, this phenomenon is not limited to Côte d'Ivoire. Most low-income countries suffer from brain drain. This hobbles national development, as many qualified people leave the country, and corrupt leaders with weak institutions and corrupt judiciaries remain in power. People lose hope in the prospect of positive change when their home regions are the scene of active conflict. *And who can blame them for wanting to protect themselves and their families?*

Higher Education

The armed conflict in Afghanistan and Côte d'Ivoire have from time to time caused universities there to shut down temporarily. Many people in those countries spent seven or eight years, or even more, trying to finish three-year degrees due to interruptions caused by conflicts. When students cannot receive timely and quality education, their prospects for a professional career inevitably suffer, so many enter the labor force without a university education. Consequently, the ambitions of many bright and talented people go to waste. This naturally creates ripple effects throughout society. Disrupted educations hinder the development of places that need that development the most. Even when things get back to normal, destroyed infrastructure must be repaired before education can proceed effectively.

Another tragic aspect of conflict-disrupted education is the sexual assaults on girls that frequently occur due to weak governance and subsequent poor law enforcement. Families want to protect their daughters from such attacks and so become reluctant to send them outside the home except for urgent reasons.

During my time in Côte d'Ivoire, armed conflict prevented many bright and ambitious young people from completing their education at the University of Cocody, Abidjan, and providing for their families. Some even had to leave the country to find refuge elsewhere. Most people think of the war in terms of death and debilitating injury, but armed conflict also leads to other long-term consequences in the realms of education, health care, and psychological wellbeing.

In Afghanistan, the armed conflict has broken the education infrastructure. Many who once looked forward to university education with hopes of a high-paying career, later on, have been left struggling to provide a basic livelihood for themselves and their families. The country now has generations without a university education. This has made many older Afghans rather oblivious to the benefits of such an education, as they have lived their entire lives without those advantages. Given that the elderly in Afghanistan receive great respect, younger Afghans often face resistance when they seek advice from their elders about their desire to obtain a Western scientific education.

Time management is yet another issue that affects many low-income countries. Deadlines do not have the same meaning there as they do in higher-income nations. In Walewale, Ghana, nobody referred to specific times; they would instead speak of sometime in the morning, around lunch, or in the evening. With the popularity of cell phones, people just call and fix the plan then and there.

On my first day in Walewale, I reached the office at eight in the morning precisely, but the office remains practically empty until 10 A.M. People took their lunch whenever they felt hungry, and people also left work whenever they wanted to. Even the director of our organization's district assembly hardly ever arrived at the office on time. For a while, I made sure that I was at the office at eight in the morning and stayed until four in the afternoon, but I eventually had to adapt to others' schedules. This laxity is a feature of rural areas and small villages, but in the largest cities, the culture is much different because of all the large private companies and international organizations that have offices there.

Bus schedules can also be erratic. Typically, they leave when they are full. In rural areas, the entire concept of clocks and time is foreign; people organize their days by the sun. They rise at dawn and begin their routines, and when the sun gets low, they move to other activities. Again, the cities are very different. In Accra and other large cities with international organizations, the concept of clock-time is more common.

When it comes to shopping in low-income countries, the price of nearly everything is negotiable. In Ghana and Afghanistan, the open markets were always busy irrespective of the time of day or day of the week. You can find beautiful textiles and traditional clothing in the shops of Kabul, Accra, and Abidjan. If the shopkeeper suspects you are a foreigner, their initial price will be higher than it would be for a local; sometimes, it can be three times the local price. Nevertheless, you will never be thought of as rude to bargain and walk away from a deal. You should never feel pressured to purchase anything. Another way to get reasonable prices is to have a local friend or colleague because they usually will know better what the going rate is and can bargain on your behalf.

Transportation

The availability and customs concerning public transport vary around the world. For instance, in Ghana and its neighboring countries, you have small vans or minibuses called tro tros. They are privately owned and travel fixed routes, although their schedules are erratic because drivers tend to wait for as many riders as they can carry. Most people depend on tro tros to get back and forth from schools, offices and other workplaces, and even just for sightseeing. They are an integral part of everyday travel. They only start moving when they are full to their capacity because the owners want to maximize their revenue per mile.

In Afghanistan, the situation is similar. The local population uses little vans for commuting to work and shopping. They are an easy and affordable way to travel; they are also faster than big buses, and sometimes drivers will alter their routes to suit each person's needs.

On average, professionals and students have a long trip to cover every day. They have to wake early, hike, or ride on unpaved roads on the way to work. The long distances often make the transition difficult for people who do not have a car or ride. As such, some people use their cars as taxis in countries like Uzbekistan, Tajikistan, and Côte d'Ivoire. This method allows students and professionals to earn a ride to their destinations early.

Simultaneously, it is an avenue for drivers to earn some money while heading to work or home. It is similar to Uber service, except that there are no applications or registrations. One only needs to stand by the roadside and flag a driver who drives by. When a price is agreed, the driver heads to the agreed location and picks up more people who are plying that route. Usually, the drivers do this when heading to or returning from work in the morning and evening. The passengers understand that they will likely pick other people who ply their route. If they desire to ride alone, they have to hire special taxis that serve only one customer per ride. Such rides are costlier than the general ride.

Interestingly, another way to easily tell a country's progress is to evaluate how often the locals abide by traffic signals. In Afghanistan and most of the West African countries that I visited; people often ignore the driving rules. They drive higher than the speed limit, and they hold no regard for pedestrians. The pedestrians have to keep their eyes on the road before crossing. Equally, the motorcyclists ride without their helmets. On the flip side, people often pay serious attention to traffic laws in developed nations. They hate to get demerit points on driving records or to be heavily fined for traffic violations. The rules are not different in developing communities. The lack of traffic cameras or efficient traffic police only makes it easier to get away with traffic violations. Succinctly put, lack of efficient execution and implementation is why people break laws.

During my years in Afghanistan and West Africa, I noticed certain customs concerning how women are seated in public transportation. In Ghana, I only rarely saw a woman sitting next to the driver in the front seat. Usually, two or even three men filled that space. Later, I learned that as per the locals, this arrangement reflects the belief that, if a woman sits next to the driver, he could become distracted by her beauty and put the passengers at risk of a collision. So, women always sit toward the back of Ghana's tro tros.

Another reason I heard for the custom was that tro tro drivers do not avoid running into livestock that strays onto the road; apparently, they prefer to kill the cows or goats rather than making a sudden swift change in the direction while driving and jeopardize the lives of people in the van. The thinking goes, if a woman were sitting next to the driver, and she witnessed a deadly collision with a cow or goat, she might shout or become so emotional that she would distract the driver.

Throughout sub-Saharan Africa, a bus driver's invitation for you to sit in the front row is a mark of respect. Most people believe that the front seat is the most comfortable, so drivers typically offer those seats to their friends and elderly men. In Afghanistan, however, bus drivers typically offer the front seats to women, believing that their male passengers may harass women passengers who sit toward the rear of the bus. That fear is evident also in the custom of providing all-female shuttles.

I have heard of incidents in which women were harassed with sexual advances from Afghan men while sitting in mixed company toward the back of a bus. Afghan society segregates the sexes strictly, so when that segregation breaks down, and men are mingling with women in close proximity, some men see this as an opportunity to harass women (and give all Afghan men a bad reputation to boot).

Most buses reserve several rows toward the back for women, minimizing the opportunities for sexual misbehavior.

Private company cars in Afghanistan have their own seating customs. Seating arrangements can differ, depending on the number of men and women passengers. As per my experience, if a car is carrying three women and one man, the man sits in front, and the women sit at the back. But if there are three men and one woman, the woman sits in front, and the men sit at the back. When you have two men and two women passengers in a private company car, either the two men will sit in front, cramped next to the driver, with the women sitting in the back, or vice versa.

As I noted before, Afghan culture maintains a high and strict level of sex segregation that extends beyond public transport to schools and sports facilities. Men and women stay apart as much as they can, mingling together only in cramped quarters. Boys and girls often study separately in Afghanistan high schools. From what I observed, it is a little bit different in their universities. The males sit at the front while the females sit at the back, or they both sit in a parallel position. Many religious leaders and professors believe that women should not sit at the front because they can distract the teachers. They can equally distract the male students sitting behind. I do not remember seeing a male between two females or vice versa in any occasion.

Some schools even draw curtains between the same class to separate the boys from the girls. I have seen and understand how this segregation leads to sexual frustration and tension between people. Afghans grow up never having the experience of interacting with the opposite sex, and the unfortunate results are evident in their adult personalities.

Finances

Few commercial transactions in Afghanistan and West Africa proceed using electronic payments, and the use of credit/debit cards is uncommon. Most people in these countries use cash for everyday purchases. In countries such as Uzbekistan, the highest currency denomination is about fifty cents, so most people carry a considerable amount of cash with them all the time. I have often seen large stacks of paper currency at local supermarkets in Uzbekistan.

At the beginning and end of the month in many African countries, many people queue up outside ATMs for hours to withdraw cash, as that is when they receive their salaries. Quite often, the ATMs run out of money, and the unfortunate people must return and wait in line again the next day.

In Afghanistan, one rarely sees an ATM in rural areas, and hardly anyone uses credit/debit cards. Afghans carry out all commercial transactions, including purchases of vehicles, in cash. Most people take their salaries in U.S. dollars rather than the local currency in Uzbekistan, Tajikistan, and Afghanistan. One reason for this is that the value of the local currency can fluctuate wildly and USD is much more trusted. If you are working in one of these countries, I advise you to carry one or two hundred dollars with you at all times, and much more if you are in a conflict-torn country. Doing so can be especially valuable during emergencies.

Stores and restaurants typically do not accept credit cards, except for luxury 5-star hotels. Also, it is recommended to carry new USD banknotes of different denominations. Sometimes, the exchange rates are also based on the unique serial numbers of USD, as some notes despite having the same value can fetch different exchange rates because of their particular serial numbers.

In Côte d'Ivoire, the biggest currency bill was 10,000 CFA franc, an equivalent of USD 20. I recall for many, this amount was very big to carry around. Many shopkeepers would not be happy if you presented them with this note and purchased only a few cheap items. Meaning they would have to give a lot of small denomination currencies as a change. So unless you don't plan on a bigger purchase, breaking the 10,000 CFA franc into smaller denominations would prove to be a lot of inconveniences.

Surprisingly, in Uzbekistan, the exchange rates were much higher in black markets compared to official money exchange shops. It was common to see people on the streets exchanging their USD for Som, the local currency of Uzbekistan. Even though it is an illegal act, it is widely practiced. It was not only a favorable rate but also if the person wants to exchange more dollars than legally allowed, then that person must buy or sell at the "black" market rate, rather than through the official/government market. In certain areas of the city in Tashkent, specific hand gestures towards strangers could also be a nonverbal way of asking them whether they can exchange the money or not.

Entertainment

When it comes to entertainment in Afghanistan, it's all about Bollywood. Many people watch these Hindi movies and enjoy their music. You can find posters of famous Bollywood actors and actresses in shops all over Afghanistan and some places in Ghana as well. Actors such as Shahrukh Khan and Amitabh Bachhan are popular all-over Central Asia. One reason for this is that Afghans feel more closely culturally related to Indian movies than American ones, as Bollywood is more family-oriented and depicts less nudity and obscene language.

In Ghana and throughout sub-Saharan Africa, Bollywood movies maintain particular popularity, but in most rural areas, people seem to prefer Nigerian or "Nollywood" movies. These films usually resonate with Ghanaians because the cultural experiences they depict are more familiar. However, when it comes to sci-fi movies, it's always Hollywood because of their superior production values in terms of graphics.

In low-income countries, the Bollywood and Nollywood film industries help to create awareness about social issues such as witch camps, overpopulation, bride price, human trafficking, ethnic discrimination, etc. These movies can influence people's thinking a great deal. So it's unfortunate that so many of them feature male characters who harass the female characters with phone calls and messages, flaunt their money, and stalk as elements of their romantic arsenals. Of course, such depictions can normalize disrespectful behavior for many viewers. Since people of all ages enjoy these movies, the movie industry is very vital in shaping local people's thinking, especially in rural areas of Africa.

In Afghanistan, censors are powerful and strict, generally prohibiting the display of any bare skin apart from the face or above the wrist of the person. On television, censorship goes for both men and women. Programs aired in Afghanistan include Afghan news and political programs, original reality TV shows, Bollywood movies, and American programs. Censors screen all movies showed on television before airing to judge them for nudity and language. No movies that promote protests against the country's political system and its human rights violations are broadcast. Despite the strict censorship of movies and television in Afghanistan, however, pirated CDs of movies and music, including pornography, are available on the black market.

Since musicians in Afghanistan fare under threat for attempting to follow their passion, many of those from Badakhshan province perform in Khorog, a neighboring city in Tajikistan. Many perform in Shughni language which is one of the Pamir languages distributed across the Gorno-Badakhshan Autonomous Region.

The music culture is much more developed and encouraged in Tajikistan, creating a sense of freedom for Afghan musicians particularly those of Badakhshan province. I recall a few Afghan colleagues, who were also musicians, performed at the "Roof of the World" festival, a yearly event across the Panj River in Khorog, Tajikistan. This festival's objective is to develop cultural exchanges between the people of central Asia, sharing their customs and traditions through music, art, and dance. It is an excellent opportunity for Afghan artists to showcase their talent without fear.

Sports and Fitness

Afghanistan's national sport is buzkashi, which many people are passionate about, especially in rural areas. Typically, they schedule the matches for Fridays and draw the attention of thousands of people. Others in Central Asia also enjoy this sport, including the Kyrgyz, Pashtuns, Kazakhs, Uzbeks, Hazaras, Tajiks, and Turkmens. In buzkashi, opposing teams of horsemen strive for possession of the headless carcass of a goat.

In Fayzabad, Badakhshan, where I lived, the enthusiasm and excitement for a buzkashi match was equivalent to a big ice hockey match in Canada or a vital cricket match in India.

Traditionally, games could last for several days, but in its more regulated tournament version, it has a limited match time. In Fayzabad, matches were staged only twice a year, so people would come from neighboring countries to compete or watch the competition. More than 200,000 spectators would watch the final match of the tournament in Fayzabad.

Unfortunately, I never saw any woman watching a buzkashi match; it's sadly become a culture where competing in and watching sports is only for men. As a foreign male, I also realized that encouraging women's participation in sports encountered the disapproval of many conservative Afghans who are resistant to change in their culture.

Earthquakes and Climate Change

Afghanistan has a mountainous terrain and experiences many earthquakes. These regularly bring tragic deaths and significant damage to property in the country. During my years in Afghanistan, I would feel or hear of an earthquake at least once every two weeks in Badakhshan. Some were severe, and some were not, but they always caused damage where they occurred.

I recall in October 2015 being in a conference when a strong earthquake shook our building. We all had to hurry outside, and the memory of people panicking and rushing to get outside during that earthquake still frightens me. It was a 7.5 magnitude centered in the mountainous Hindu Kush region, about 45 miles from our location in Fayzabad.

According to the UN, it was estimated that at least 399 people were killed from the impact of that earthquake. Though all of our colleagues were unhurt, the experience of watching people panic and shout with fear while the earth below us was trembling and the buildings were almost swinging, taught me that despite having differences in nationalities and religion, we all behave similarly when in a close encounter with death. I recall some were praying; some were crying, some were confounded and remained still with fear. Even the bravest ones had distress on their face. Those couple of minutes still remain a very impactful episode of my life thus far.

Much of the death and damage in rural areas results from the inferior materials and construction techniques that people use to build their houses there. Due to the economic situation, people typically build their houses out of mud or other materials that cannot survive the impact of an earthquake.

Earthquakes also often trigger landslides because most of Afghanistan is now virtually treeless due to national and some international logging mafias that have stripped the countryside of firewood. According to Water Resource Management, Afghanistan now has less than 0.5 percent of its area covered by forest, down from more than 3 percent in 1980. The loose soil on hillsides causes hundreds of landslide-related casualties each year.

I remember an incident from May 2014, when I was in the area of Badakhshan. A landslide occurred on a Friday in the district of Argo. Because Fridays are religious holidays in Afghanistan, most people were in their homes, and many of them died there during the landslide. Initially, reports estimated that as many as 2,000 had died, but later estimates were revised downward to about 400. In many of these tragedies, the local media and district governments often overestimate the casualties, as this brings more attention to the incident and the national government mounts a faster and more extensive response.

Climate change has caused several negative consequences in many countries, and natural disasters and unpredictable weather conditions contribute to the development woes of low-income countries. Even though global warming will eventually affect people everywhere, in some places I have been, the effects are already gruesome.

In sub-Saharan Africa, for example, untimely rains and droughts are unfortunately frequent. Once when I was in Walewale, two big storms that came one after another destroyed the roofs of many houses, schools, and other buildings. These storms were so intense that a 100-year-old tree crashed on a group of people, killing 10 of them. After those storms, monies that had been earmarked for development initiatives were instead used to rehabilitate government buildings. This happens often; development priorities suffer in the wake of natural disasters and armed conflict.

Many of the soils in sub-Saharan Africa have lost much of what little fertility they originally had because farmers have not replaced the nutrients that decades of crops absorbed from them. Many farmers were also forced by the colonial powers to grow indigo, since indigo planting was more commercially profitable due to the demand for blue dye in Europe. So, in their current state, these soils cannot support agriculture adequate for the nutrition of the region's population. Progressive declines in soil moisture have increased the need for irrigation, which increases the soil's salinity and eventually leads to ever-smaller yields and even desertification. This vicious cycle has dire implications for the region's food production.

In Afghanistan, I was very fortunate to visit an area in the northeast known as the Wakhan Corridor. If you look at a map of Afghanistan, it is the skinny arm extending between Tajikistan to the north, Pakistan to the south, and a bit of China to the east. Its average elevation is about 4,000 meters (about 13,000 feet), it has one of Earth's most punishing climates and topographies, and many believe that it is the most impoverished area in Afghanistan. Parts of the Hindu Kush and Pamir mountains, with their alpine valleys, stretch across the Wakhan Corridor from the province of Badakhshan to the headwaters of the Amu Darya River in the Pamirs. It is more than 200 kilometers (about 125 miles) long and 20- 60 kilometers (about 12-37 miles) wide, covering a total area of about 10,300 square kilometers (about 4,000 square miles). The Corridor, and in particular its eastern end in the Pamir Knot, has always been one of the most remote and least accessible regions of Afghanistan.

In Wakhan, the average life expectancy is less than 35 years, and one in four children die before they reach their first birthday. Years of war have sorely affected the people and wildlife of Afghanistan, but the Corridor's isolation has mitigated those effects there. Only about 12,000 people live there, mostly in pockets isolated from each other.

The area is inhabited by two main ethnic groups, the Wakhi and the Kyrgyz. The Wakhi often have two homes, one for winter and another one for summer months. The latter is usually made of stone. The Kyrgyz are more nomadic, living in semi-portable yurt tents made of Felt. They move their homes and animals to different valleys depending on the season.

Livestock farming is essentially the only commercial activity. They trade sheep, goats, and yaks to merchants from Pakistan or other parts of Afghanistan for clothing, food, and necessities they can't produce themselves at these remote high-altitude locations that they call home. Due to climate change, the amount of snow the region receives every year has been decreasing. This further affects the habitation and vegetation, which is unfortunate for the livestock and in turn, for the human population generally.

The area is so isolated that it takes about four to five days to drive from Badakhshan's provincial capital of Fayzabad to Wakhan. Driving from Fayzabad to Wakhan via the Shuhada district of Badakhshan is about 180 km, but due to the mountainous nature and the condition of the road, it can take up to 4 or 5 days of travel. My pleasure and satisfaction to see the success of development projects such as the Micro Hydel Plant and other irrigation initiatives was tempered by the effects of climate change that the area is suffering. The people of Wakhan were very skeptical about their future due to their warming climate.

There are hardly any other organizations that have a presence in Wakhan except Aga Khan Foundation, as it's so isolated. Any group that attempts to operate there faces very high operations and logistics costs. The area does have enormous potential for tourism, but the country's reputation for security and the effects of climate change limit that potential. As a whole, the region, is like heaven for mountaineers and hikers with its lofty peaks. The area's isolation also allows traders and the Taliban from Pakistan to pass through with absolutely no border control.

Exercise is needed to offset the traditional Afghan diet. Afghan cuisine tends to be very salty and meat-oriented. With modern Afghans getting less exercise, this further exacerbates existing health issues. I met many Afghans with health conditions, and many look much older than their chronological age, mainly due to their diet and sedentary lifestyle, as well as the fretful conditions perpetuated by decades of armed conflicts.

Many international organizations have created initiatives to increase awareness of healthy lifestyles and diets, but cultural habits can be very difficult to change, especially in societies that treasure their traditions. For instance, I recall an initiative that introduced barley flour for making bread. Most Afghans did not like the taste of barley mixed with white flour, however, and remained loyal to their traditional white flour. In Ghana, cuisine options are similarly limited, with few vegetables, and this results in childhood nutritional deficiencies.

Children in sub-Saharan Africa grow up with a very close connection to the wild environment that surrounds them, so their immunity against endemic disease must be very strong for them to survive. Unfortunately, many die due to poisoning from eating wild berries and other fruits.

In this part of the world, a lack of knowledge can be deadly. Throughout my visits to rural villages in this part of Africa, I often saw various kinds of berries hanging from trees. Usually, the locals advised against them or any other thing that they themselves don't consume. Especially dangerous, I was told, were a kind of red berries with a black spot called Abrus precatorius, commonly known as jequirity bean or rosary pea. Given the limited medical facilities in sub-Saharan Africa, it is always best to eat only the native foods that the locals also eat.

The ignorance of the effects of consuming certain local crops can cause severe damage to the human body. At one point, I heard of an outbreak of a kind of paralysis in the Wakhan Corridor. Eventually, experts traced the outbreak to the consumption of a type of grass pea. When eaten in small quantities, this grass pea is harmless, but the Wakhans had started eating it as a major part of their diet. Over a three-month period, then, toxins in the pea can cause lathyrism, a permanent paralysis below the knees in adults, as well as brain damage in children. Fortunately, doctors discovered the connection between the pea and lathyrism fairly quickly, and the Wakhans have since followed their advice. They now use the grass pea for feeding the donkeys in the Wakhan region.

Clean Water Shortage

One of the most challenging aspects of living in sub-Saharan Africa is adapting to the shortage of fresh and clean water. I lived in Walewale in northeastern Ghana, and my house had the usual large water tank on its roof; it supplied water to our taps (when it had any water in it). About five times a month, a man would bring us two barrels of water on a donkey cart. With the help of his little son, it would take an hour to fill the tank, and for this, the cost was about $4. In an area where most people earn only about $100 a month, this was very expensive. So many people carried their own water from village wells, and depending on the distance, this could take them as much as two or three hours every day. The water is never colorless, and with every storm in the village, the water quality would deteriorate further.

Harmattan is a season in West Africa that occurs between the end of November and the middle of March. It brings a characteristic dry and dusty trade wind out of the northeast from the Sahara Desert and blows out over the Gulf of Guinea. This time of the year is relatively cold, and because of the dry conditions, water delivery is more expensive than usual. Worse yet, harmattan negatively affects water quality because of all the sand blowing into it. As bad as water quality can be, water scarcity can be a much bigger issue in some African villages, where people sometimes have to travel for days to other villages to fetch water when the rains are late.

In certain areas, even when water is available, it is still of very poor quality and unfit for drinking. Wells can be contaminated by disease, and water pipelines often break during storms. I witnessed many villages in Afghanistan and in Ghana that were dealing with waterborne disease. For instance, during a field visit to a village near Walewale, I saw some children who were going blind due to an infectious disease called trachoma because of water from a well contaminated by an animal carcass.

In Afghanistan, cholera outbreaks are common because of a lack of latrines. People in many areas defecate near drinking-water reservoirs. In some locations, the available water contains toxic minerals leached from local geological formations, making it impure and a hazard to drinking. Due to water scarcity, however, people still consume it and therefore suffer from whatever diseases it causes. Low water quality, along with crowded living conditions, also leads to frequent outbreaks of skin diseases such as scabies, psoriasis, and eczema.

According to the World Health Organization (WHO), water-related diseases cause the death of over 3.4 million people annually. This makes it the foremost and most dangerous cause of disease and death all over the world. There is an urgent need to pay close attention to Water and Sanitation Programs. (WASH)

Alcohol

In Ghana and Côte d'Ivoire, alcohol is freely available as in high-income countries; one can witness groups in the evening at the outside stalls having their favorite beer with roasted beef or chicken kebabs. Rural areas can have problems with alcoholism, but they are nothing compared to British binge drinking. Many of the Africans I know are responsible drinkers.

Throughout the years, I have encountered far fewer drunks in Africa than I have in the U.S., the UK, and Canada. African culture encourages responsible drinking for their youth. There are always exceptions, of course, but even at the African night clubs, people still seem to have their senses under control by the end of the evening.

In Kabul, life as an expatriate worker can be quite dull sometimes, as one is mostly inside one's residence or compound. Expatriates generally spend their social time visiting the homes of other expatriates in Kabul. People have underground parties where alcohol and several kinds of drugs are available. There is a list of people invited, and so it's only for selected people, mostly foreign workers with few Afghan men. It's easier to invite another expatriate worker to these parties, as they are more trusted, and also, all expatriates have gone through a security clearance before entering Afghanistan.

This list exists mainly because of the safety issue and knowing the person who will be attending. Attending such a party can make you forget that you are in a war zone in a very conservative country. Many expatriate houses are very comfortable with hired help that serve as cleaners and cooks. They take care of all the household chores, are inexpensive, and easy to find.

At the Kabul airport, customs officers may allow each foreigner to bring two bottles of alcoholic beverages into the country. But not all foreigners are created equal. Sometimes, the officers check the name and nationality of each individual entering Afghanistan after first inspecting their luggage. If you have a non-Islamic name and carry a passport from a non-Islamic country, the customs officers will allow you to bring the two bottles in with you.

But as per other expatriates, if you have an Islamic name and show a passport from a non-Islamic country, you could be in trouble if you try to bring alcohol into the country. This selectively enforced policy sometimes creates severe problems for the person carrying the alcohol. Many times, customs inspections fail to find alcohol in one's luggage, so, many expatriates bring alcohol in. But if the officers find alcohol hidden in their luggage, the person caught often becomes the target of shouting and embarrassment by immigration officers. They will tell the individual that she or he is an embarrassment to Islam and that they tarnish the religion, and this process is usually much harsher for women than for men.

In the minds of many conservative Afghans, a Muslim woman, including foreign nationals, drinking alcohol is taboo, even though they might not openly admit this. So, after being confronted with an accusation that one is jeopardizing the name of Islam, most incoming Muslims are forced to surrender their wine or spirits. Of course, many immigration officers drink alcohol themselves, but most would never admit it. I once had an immigration officer request for me to bring a bottle of alcohol for them on my return. All this depends on the mood of the immigration officers. If they are contented and happy, they might let this slip by. But if you wind up with an officer who's having a bad day, you better be on your guard.

This situation is much more challenging during the month of Ramadan, as fasting Afghans tend to be fatigued and sometimes impertinent. During Ramadan, it pays to be polite and compliant at immigration and when you're out and about in general.

Some Afghans skirt the ban on alcohol by asking expatriates to bring alcohol in for them. Many in the larger cities do drink alcohol at parties with mostly expatriates, but very seldom have I seen alcohol in rural areas. Some during official or tourism visits outside the country consume alcohol, especially in India, UAE, and Tajikistan. Asking an Afghan person if they drink alcohol in Afghanistan is a very sensitive topic.

Gun Culture

Afghanistan is the biggest market for illegal guns in the world. Even the small town of Fayzabad has an open market for guns. Ostensibly, these are hunting weapons, but in fact, they are military arms, and you need no special licenses to purchase them. While Afghans are required to obtain police permission to buy a weapon, the statute is rarely enforced.

Most tribal leaders and the Pashtun population of southern Afghanistan keep guns in their households for hunting and personal protection. This gun culture is prevalent and has been in Afghanistan for decades now. The country has a long tradition of gun ownership, and a wide range of firearms - from pistols and shotguns to fully automatic weapons - are readily available. Marriage ceremonies and countless other celebrations in Kabul are not complete without volleys of bullets being shot into the air. The sight of even little boys carrying rifles is troublingly common.

Decades ago, the American government showered the mujahedeen (whom they considered freedom fighters) with guns and other weapons to fight the invading Soviet army. This practice continues today, although the enemy now is the Taliban. For their part, the Taliban receive their weaponry from Pakistan, Iran, and other terrorist groups in Middle Eastern countries. Ironically, most of those arms are also American, captured by terrorists in Syria or Iraq.

During my stay in Côte d'Ivoire, I saw the military carried AK-47s and other advanced firearms in supermarkets and common public places. The region has so much weaponry remaining from years of conflict that the policy of disarming militants and rebels has significantly failed. Because guns have a useful life of about 100 years, many of today's weapons entered Africa decades ago during the continent's various civil wars. Just like the American policy of providing weapons to the Afghan mujahedeen that backfired when the Taliban got their hands on those weapons, the French Government was the source of many weapons in West Africa, unfortunately now in the possession of rebels and terrorists.

Although tracing the ebbs and flows of the arms markets in conflict-torn areas can be difficult, it is easy to see the harm that these weapons inflict on civilian populations. The years of conflict in Afghanistan have led to many mental health issues; people are more aggressive than they used to be, so otherwise, minor accidents often lead to fatal stabbings and shootings. Even elderly men are often the perpetrators. They consider giving deference as a sign of weakness, and needless death is often the result of neighborhood arguments. During my time in Afghanistan, I saw and heard of a terrible number of stabbings, a distressing level of drug addiction, and a general lack of law and order.

Journalism

I personally believe that national journalists in Afghanistan have among the riskiest jobs of anyone there. Afghanistan has one of the world's most complex and contested information environments. At times, it can be challenging to tell the difference between propaganda, intelligence, and journalism. Some journalists who covered Taliban activities were accused of treason or arrested by the National Directorate of Security (NDS), while others have been kidnapped, beaten, or assassinated by Taliban insurgents.

Afghan journalists face threats from both sides: the insurgent groups and the Afghan National Security Forces (ANSF). Several of these brave individuals were killed while providing or trying to provide information to the general media. Many international journalists also work in Afghanistan, but they are not as exposed to danger as the local journalists. They are, however, sometimes blocked from visiting certain areas and reporting on specific activities.

In Tajikistan and Uzbekistan, the governments control the activities of journalists even more than that of Afghanistan. They sometimes confiscate journalists' cameras and recording devices when the journalists leave the country, especially if they suspect that the journalists might report on human rights violations.

The Uzbekistan government will not allow any development agency to do any work concerning human rights without prior and explicit approval. This is presumably in response to the many reports in the international media about Uzbekistan's inhumane treatment of opposition parties and religious groups. Not surprisingly, the local media never even mentions the political opposition. Most Uzbeks and Tajiks have learned to live with the fact that personal prosperity in the country absolutely depends on supporting the government and never protesting anything about it.

Safety and Security

Afghanistan has many shopping malls and markets to visit and some very high-profile restaurants, but all are very vulnerable to an attack. During my time in Afghanistan, one of the big cases was a suicide bomber who also killed several people, including a three-year-old in the city's most prestigious hotel. The hotel thought that it had plenty of security; each person who wanted to get in was checked at least three times before entering the hotel. Yet the Taliban member who mounted the attack got past them all, disguised as a guest. Many attacks occur because someone within the facility passes secret security information to the Taliban. Reasons for this cooperation with the Taliban vary from financial to social coercion or blackmail. Kidnapping is a common crime committed by the Taliban, and the ransom could be providing confidential information such as hotel security protocols.

Most cities in Afghanistan have a curfew at about six or seven in the evening; this is especially true of smaller cities. You see very few people outside at that time of day, and streetlights can be very uncommon in smaller Afghan cities; I strongly advise not to go out after dinner. In Accra, Abidjan, and even smaller cities in Western Africa, on the other hand, more people tend to be out and about unless recent violence has made walking about after dark too risky. Impending elections can also have that effect; at such times, the local military rarely approves of anyone being out during the evening. Otherwise, many street vendors can be seen until late evening in the hope to sell their products to make enough money for their families.

Because of the risk associated with dining at high-quality restaurants in Kabul, most expatriates order food at home from those restaurants. Practically every organization operating in Afghanistan has a security advisor that employees can consult about safe and risky areas and establishments.

Of course, some foreigners still go to dangerous places that security experts had advised them to avoid. This is very common and unfortunate, as some expatriates have paid dearly for not complying with security protocols. Such misfortune usually results from a feeling of false heroism, wanting to demonstrate that one is not afraid of security threats. Such behavior is unintelligent, to say the least; you should always follow all security protocols. If you were to be kidnapped, your organization would be in a very tough position, as they may be forced to pay your ransom from funds that had been earmarked for development purposes.

Restaurants in Kabul have segregated areas for women and families. Afghan men never eat with unmarried women in restaurants unless they are related. So if you are a foreign man who wants to dine with a local Afghan woman at a restaurant, you need to bring along other female expatriate colleagues; one-on-one dining will definitely lead to trouble and shame for the woman. The rule applies even to foreign men and women. Unmarried man-woman couples in Afghan restaurants almost always attract uncomfortable stares from others. The main exception is when the other diners owe some special respect to the male diner at a one-on-one meal. If no one is staring at you while dining that translates to respect they have for you.

In sub-Saharan Africa, however, I never was made uncomfortable by dining with someone of either sex. When it comes to dining out, Ghanaian culture is very similar to that of North America; it's just two people having a meal together. Ghanaians and Ivorian's alike tend to be much more liberal when it comes to interactions with the opposite sex.

In conflict areas, you need to know the drill for going through security checkpoints, which you will find in malls, restaurants, hotels, and airports. You will go through many metal detectors and body searches before you are allowed to enter. Yet even with all those expensive security facilities and gadgets, many attacks still occur.

For example, Kabul airport has several layers of security for passengers. They begin outside the airport while you are still in your car. You might be miles away from the airport when you encounter the first checkpoint. You will be asked to stop your car, get out, submit to a body check, and go through a metal detector while uniformed personnel inspects your car for bombs or any other threats. The second checkpoint also occurs outside the airport, where passengers leave their baggage. Here you go through a metal detector, submit to a pat-down, and have your luggage thoroughly scanned. A few meters further, you encounter the third checkpoint, which consists of a pat-down and a verification of your passport and ticket. The fourth check of baggage, tickets, and passports, also occurs before you enter the airport proper. To enter the airport building, you must submit to a more in-depth security check, which involves a search of the contents of your baggage and your wallet, another pat-down, and questions about your travel.

At this point, sometimes, if the airport staff suspects that you are non-Muslim and they are feeling surly, they may harass you with further security procedures. If you are traveling with a female colleague, expect them to ask you about your relationship with her. It would be best if you answered all their questions with a calm demeanor.

After all that, you might think you're done, but you would be wrong. When you get your boarding pass at the airline counter and check all your baggage, you must go through yet another security check. Going through immigration involves another check (passport), and after that, security personnel will open your laptop and tell you to remove your shoes and anything else they deem suspicious. Airline personnel carries out the final security checks just before you board your flight.

As per other female expatriates, Afghan security personnel sometimes harass foreign women, but there is no point complaining at the airport, as most of the Afghan men working in immigration generally find such harassment amusing. If you need to file a complaint, do so only outside the airport.

Despite all the security checkpoints at the Kabul airport (eight or nine in most cases) and all the time they consume, the facility has been subjected to many attacks in recent years. Most of them depended on infiltrators who have inside information that they then provide to the Taliban or other insurgent groups. This kind of corruption is the reason why the Taliban still has a strong presence in 50 to 60 percent of the country. Afghanistan's endemic poverty leads many to switch their allegiance from the government to the Taliban.

One aspect of working in a conflict area that is the same as anywhere else is that everyone keeps their phones with them all the time. The difference, of course, is that having your phone on your person could be a matter of life or death. International organizations regularly provide security updates about active fighting in nearby areas, alerting you to stay away from those areas. Some organizations require their foreign employees to reply to a text message every day before a certain time; that way, they can keep tabs on where their people are and how they are doing. Always obey these security policies.

Even when employees leave the country on vacation, many organizations expect them to keep their phones with them, turned on and charged up, in case an emergency occurs back in the conflict zone. This is particularly true for those in upper management positions. They need to stay up to date on the situation back at their stations.

An employee might not always face harsh consequences for not meeting a work deadline, but when it comes to security noncompliance, or even worse, a breach, employees always face questions from their line managers and/or security staff. A kidnapping or other serious security lapse can damage an organization's reputation around the world. Top candidates for key positions avoid organizations with a poor security record. So, every security protocol must be followed to the letter.

Surprising though it may seem, Internet availability and usage are still not common everywhere in the world. Some areas may have availability but poor signal strength. Most residents of rural Africa and Afghanistan use Wi-Fi or cellular dongles to connect to the Internet. Private connections in many areas tend to be expensive, so most residents of West African cities surf the internet at Internet cafés. Economically prosperous people have Wi-Fi connections at home, but this is still uncommon.

These internet cafés are also the birthplace of many spam and scam emails. In them, you can almost always see at least one person typing and forwarding spam messages. Many also use the Internet to develop romantic relationships with people outside the country, which they see as opportunities to emigrate. Many do this out of economic desperation. In my experience in Afghanistan, technology and the Internet are more advanced than in West Africa; this is probably because of all the foreign missions and delegations that have been in the country for decades. Views of pornographic Internet sites in Afghanistan are as high as other areas globally, including in the most conservative areas.

To maintain your personal security in Afghanistan, you must not only keep a low profile in public but also adopt a very conservative approach. Publicly staring at a local woman can get you into trouble if any of her male relatives see you. In all my time overseas, I never saw a man approach an unknown female on the street. All romantic exchanges occur in private and sometimes secret settings; phones and emails play an important role in establishing romantic relationships.

The conservative culture of Afghanistan is evident even in the way that the population furnishes their apartments in high-rise buildings. Most people either paint their windows black or never open their curtains, as looking down on one's neighbors from on high is considered an invasion of privacy.

During my initial days in Afghanistan, I satisfied my desire for fresh air by opening the window of my second-floor office, only to be surprised by a small barrage of pebbles and stones being thrown at the window by passersby. This confused me at first, but I kept the window open. When the assault by the small projectiles failed to relent, I sought advice from my colleague, who rushed in and closed the window. This colleague told me that I should not open, and especially not look out of a window. People assume that an open window indicates the presence of a peeping Tom. Blackened windows also reflect laws passed during the Taliban rule. Back then, the religious police forced all women off the streets of Kabul and ordered the population to blacken their windows so that women would not be visible from outside.

Most buildings that I saw in Kabul had a safe room. It is a strong, hidden room where people can safely conceal themselves during terrorist invasions. The safe rooms are often built in the basement, and they usually contain contingency materials for an emergency. It is also possible to call for help or communicate with the world from these rooms. They are common in embassies, hotels, and similar buildings. International staff is advised to head to the nearest safe room the instant there is an emergency. This is why they should keep their identification documents with them at all times.

Threats

When it comes to traveling within the provinces of Afghanistan, the UN frequently provides airplane, and sometimes helicopter, transport for the staff of international organizations. Helicopter travel can be essential in administering aid, as they can land anywhere during weather emergencies or security threats. UN airplanes have been a frequent target of the Taliban in Afghanistan, so when they fly over Taliban-controlled territory or otherwise detect a threat, they usually will fly at a very low altitude to avoid detection by Taliban radar, which often precedes a rocket attack. Pilots during World War II developed this technique, known as "nap of the earth."

In Kabul, threats against high-profile hotels are common. Many of them have suffered attacks by insurgents, resulting in many deaths of locals and foreigners. More recently, some hotels have avoided openly identifying themselves as such, so one must rely on insiders' knowledge to know where the major hotels are situated. These hotels maintain excellent security protocols most of the time, such as checking guests in outside the hotel on the sidewalk. From the street, some of the most luxurious hotels in Kabul look like shabby old buildings, but that is just a ruse to protect them from violent attacks.

Winters in Afghanistan can be very harsh, especially in rural areas. People living in the countryside usually reside in mud-brick or concrete houses with no central heating, which can be very uncomfortable when temperatures drop to below -25°C (about -13°F). Instead, people rely on Bukharis, which are a traditional kind of space heater. Bukhari's can burn either charcoal, wood, or oil and have chimneys. Consequently, Bukhari's not only pollute the outdoor air with smoke but also kill people by carbon monoxide poisoning when they are damaged or not set up properly. Since people usually use their Bukharis in the evenings, some unfortunate individuals never wake up again after going to sleep.

International staff risks their lives a lot when they work in conflict zones. Apart from being potential targets of terrorist attacks, they are also vulnerable to natural disasters. Their SUV cars are sometimes driven on mountains and unpaved roads. At other times, they have to carry their bags on donkeys and other livestock as they hike on mountains because there are no roads to their destination. I lost two local colleagues on one such occasion. They were trying to cross a river on a rickety boat that sank halfway. Development workers genuinely deserve a lot of commendation for putting their lives at risk to better other people's lives.

Rest and Recreation Leave

Anyone who has worked in conflict zones knows that the concept of vacation days does not usually apply while you are in the country. You are paid to work every day that you are in the country of your mission. Most international organizations, however, do have policies for rest and recreation (R&R) leave. These typically involve full pay for a defined number of days per weeks spent in hazardous, stressful, or otherwise difficult situations. The policies usually cover all international deployed staff but sometimes also cover the domestic staff of higher management levels.

Generally, one is eligible for R&R that is usually 5 days after every 12 weeks in the country, although different organizations have different policies. Most people take their R&R in nearby countries. From Afghanistan, many people choose to visit Dubai, Delhi, Islamabad, Istanbul, or a city in Southeast Asia. In those cities, expatriate staff can freely walk the streets and even visit pubs, bars, and restaurants, which many could not do back in Afghanistan. R&R is also an opportunity for the young expatriate staff to meet and travel with their partners. Most organizations provide a generous R&R allowance, so most expatriates spend their R&R leave in nice hotels and spend more freely.

I recall my first R&R in London. I was delighted to walk anywhere I pleased after almost five months of being confined to the residential compound in Fayzabad, Badakhshan in Afghanistan. It was such a pleasant change to walk around freely and talk to anyone. For many expatriate women, the change must be even sweeter, as their behavior and dress in Afghanistan were much more constrained than mine and other men's. Expatriate women who have children back home generally go back to their native countries instead of cashing out their R&R allowance as extra savings. R&Rs are usually a time for foreign staff to relax and recuperate from all the stress they must endure. The leave is good for their mental health. Everyone must report their R&R travel plans to their respective organizations, so their co-workers will know where they are in case an emergency arises while they are away.

The ability to stay alone is a survival trait that one must cultivate for development missions. It will be required when one moves to a new city within one's country and meets new people. The faces will appear strange, and it can be challenging to recognize or make friends with anyone. It is much more complicated when the development mission is in a different country, especially a war zone, miles away from home. The local office staff is usually hospitable and friendly to foreigners. Despite this, a person on such missions will have to cope with loneliness in the evenings when the local staff have returned to their families. One may resort to working out, watching movies, or learning a new language.

On average, foreign workers are expected to work longer hours than local workers in a conflict zone. This is partly because foreign workers are not in a familiar location. They have no friends or families to tend to, and their work is all that they have in the environment. The course and nature of their work is usually faster than those who work in non-conflict countries. Their local partners sometimes work late into the night or remain available on the phone after regular work hours. This should not be exploited; however, their time has to be respected. The locals must get back to their families and perform their usual responsibilities.

As a foreign staff, it is wise to show the local workers that that one understands the value of family to them, and would not overburden them. Precisely, they are not expected to work at the same pace as the foreign workers. The locals are often inspired to work with anyone who bears such notions and tries to make the work system convenient for the local staff.

Pressures and deadlines are among the dirtiest sides of working in a conflict country like Afghanistan. It is impossible to attend social events or amusement centers like one would in other countries. One is confined to a straight-line movement: from the residence to the workplace, from the workplace back to the residence. Each day does not appear particularly different from the other; it is sedentary, and there are the same tasks to do every day. The tight deadlines and pressures can reflect on the behavior of the other staff, but it should not be taken personally. Stress, heavy workload, pressure, and insecurity are enough to burden anyone's mind.

Fig. 1 On a Bactrian camel in Wakhan, Badakhshan in Afghanistan.

Fig. 2 Wakhan, Badakhshan, Afghanistan

Fig. 3 Wakhan, Badakhshan, Afghanistan

Fig. 4 Landslide in Argo, Badakhshan, Afghanistan

Fig. 5 Game of Buzkashi being played in Fayzabad, Badakhshan

Fig. 6 Aftermath of Earthquake in Fayzabad, Afghanistan

Fig. 7 Lunch during a monitoring visit to Wakhan, Afghanistan

Fig. 8 Primary classroom in Walewale, Ghana

Fig. 9 Outside classroom in Wulugu, Ghana

Fig. 10 Primary classroom in rural Afghanistan

Chapter 3.

Dating and Marriage Culture

Throughout the world, weddings mark the commencement of family life, clearly a reason to celebrate for the couple, their families, and their friends. Many countries have unique customs and traditions surrounding the marriage ceremony.

In many low-income countries, arranged marriages are widespread. This means that families and social circles largely decide who will marry whom. Couples are often introduced to each other by their parents or other relatives.

For many people in high-income countries, the concept of an arranged marriage is somewhat like a blind date. But in this case, one must decide whether or not to marry the other person after only a few meetings. The concept of living together before marriage does not exist in Afghanistan, Tajikistan, or Uzbekistan. In some West African countries, living together before marriage is not unknown, but it is still not very common. Most unmarried couples who live together hide this from their relatives.

In high-income countries, most people would never allow their families or friends to arrange their marriages; this practice is viewed as a kind of abuse. What I have learned, though, is that most couples are not forced into arranged marriages. They usually have a choice in the matter, and increasing numbers of parents realize that forcing their sons and daughters into marriage will not make their offspring happy. The custom of arranged marriage has been prevalent for centuries in Asia and Africa. Most of these marriages are within the same ethnicity, tribe, and religion—sometimes even between cousins.

Interestingly, the divorce rate among arranged marriages in Asian and many African countries is incredibly low compared to that of Europeans and North Americans. This is likely due to the stigma of divorce in these countries. Couples are under pressure to make their marriage work. The communities also ensure that people are matched according to their values and background, rather than physical attraction. The majority of marriages do not break up as the relationship is based on shared common values, not the mere outward appearance. However, little is said about abusive relationships.

In Uzbekistan, when a young man and his family go to meet a presumptive fiancée and her parents, the young woman's family always serves the traditional tea. In this ritual, the amount of tea that the young woman pours into the young man's cup indicates how interested she is in marrying him. If she pours only a little tea into his cup, she is saying that she wants him to ask for more—that is, to stay with her. But if she fills his cup to the brim, she is saying that she is not very interested in marrying him. He should drink the tea and respectfully leave.

Most Afghan women marry between the ages of 18 and 25. Because of the threat of violence in the country in recent years, women are seen as being particularly vulnerable to abuse. Afghan culture deals with that threat by encouraging women to marry when they are very young. The culture in general accords more respect to married women than to the unmarried, and a married woman receives the protection of her husband's family.

The Afghan Civil Code asserts that a Muslim male can marry a non-Muslim female; however, it does not permit a Muslim female's marriage with a non-Muslim male. Although some foreign and non-Muslim men have married Afghan women, they had to convert to Islam and marry the woman, also dating is not part of Afghan culture.

On the other hand, Afghan law has no problem with Afghan men marrying foreign women. Afghan men can have as many as four wives, as polygamy is legal in Afghanistan. Many Afghans and Pakistanis marry within each other's communities, as the Pashtun culture is similar on both sides of the border. Another factor at play in these marriages is the large number of Afghan refugees in Pakistan. The relatively open border between Afghanistan and Pakistan also facilitates this situation. If one speaks Pashtun fluently, it's very easy to cross the border from Pakistan into Afghanistan.

Since Afghans expect women to adapt to their husband's culture, it is preferable for foreign women to accept their values and religion than for Afghan women to accept foreign values. This reflects the patriarchal culture and religion that the two countries share.

Children almost always carry their father's name and follow their father's religion. This tradition comes from the belief that one should spread one's religion and that the more followers a religion has, the stronger it will be. Many couples in Afghanistan have large families, thinking they are doing God's will by spreading the religion. This, in turn, leads to greater poverty and other social problems, as many don't have the resources to care for and educate their children properly but conceive and raise them nonetheless, for the purpose of spreading their faith.

Dowries and the Bride Price

Many societies in Africa and Asia observe the practices of dowry and bridal price. When marriages are arranged, an exchange of resources displays the status of the families involved. Dowries are money or other valuable resources that the bride's family gives to the groom during or after the wedding. Although the practice is now illegal in most countries, many ignore the law. Sometimes, a groom's family will demand a dowry at the wedding, which often causes ill will between the families.

During the colonial period in lands once ruled by Great Britain, dowries were mandatory, especially in South Asia and some parts of Africa. British law prohibited women from owning any property at all, which resulted in all their wealth going to their new husbands. Later, this practice devolved into an opportunity for grooms and their families to greedily extort wealth from bridal families.

Even now, when women can legally own property in most low-income countries, the practice is still widespread. Grooms' demands for dowries result in many women being unable to marry, and some go to the extreme of committing suicide for the shame that this brings. The demand for dowries is so common that new parents begin accumulating one as soon as they give birth to a daughter—it's not all that different than how parents in high-income countries begin saving for their children's college education from an early age.

With dowries, however, the situation is more extreme. Some people have to sell their land and take out loans to meet the dowry demands of the groom. No wonder most people are happier at the birth of a boy than of a girl. The practice of dowry can make daughters a burden for many parents. Sometimes, when the dowry demands of a groom's family are modest, the bride's family will give more than they can afford just to save face in the community. Educated people all over the world have decried the practice of dowry, and we have seen strong social movements against it, yet, unfortunately, it still prevails in certain countries. Perhaps with the upcoming generation learning about equality between the sexes, this practice will diminish with time.

In both Ghana and Afghanistan, the concept is reversed, and people refer to it as the "bride price." Here, a groom's family will give money or other valuable assets to the bride or her family. In Western and most of Sub-Saharan Africa, the bride price is a payment that grooms must make before they can marry. The amount can vary, according to the means of the groom and his family, and is often paid in cattle or goats. Negotiating the bride price is a serious matter before the marriage. It typically precedes the other arrangements for the wedding, and if it is not paid in full, the wedding may be canceled. Should a wife run away or behave badly during the marriage, the husband is entitled to reclaim the bride price.

The tradition of the bride price can have enormously destructive effects when young men cannot pay it. In Afghanistan, one of the cooks at our residential compound was already beyond the traditional marriage age and could not get married due to the high bride price. In rural Badakhshan, Afghanistan, the going rate for a bride price was $15,000, depending on the family. As many men from lower socioeconomic classes cannot afford the price, much sexual frustration ensues. Income inequality exacerbates that situation, as polygamy is legal and affluent men can afford several wives, further tipping the balance between single men and women.

Bride price and polygamy combine to leave many young Afghan men involuntarily unmarried and celibate. This frustration can embolden them to harass women, sometimes leading to violent sexual assaults. The imbalance also benefits Taliban recruitment, with young men believing that their participation will bring them the financial means to get married and start a family eventually.

Moreover, with males and females segregated in public, and many unhappy single men and women, the atmosphere of sexual tension intensifies. Online chatrooms seem to be the only way of interacting with the opposite sex. When men do find a woman to chat with online, they do not have to abide by the strict conservative culture in which they grew up, and they often express themselves in vulgar or inappropriate ways.

Many Afghan men frequent online dating sites originating in Tajikistan. Since the language is similar, many Afghans find Tajik women attractive. Unfortunately, some Afghans consider Tajikistan's capital, Dushanbe, a hub for wealthy Afghans to revel in the nightlife and sex tourism, as alcohol is permitted there. This gives a bad name to Afghans who travel to Dushanbe for reasons other than sex tourism.

Customs, Ceremonies, and Celebrations

Due to significant French, British, and American influence, many young people in the major cities of Afghanistan and West Africa enjoy Western cuisines, such as pizza and hamburgers. Fast-food chains similar to McDonald's or Burger King enjoy reputations as high-end restaurants where families go on special occasions. In West Africa, people take their dates to these fast-food eateries to create a good impression.

In most Asian and African cultures, families spend a lot of money on weddings, so they can become a huge financial burden. In Indian culture, the celebration typically lasts for several days; traditional events happen during the day and evening. In Ghana, marriage involves a feast during the day, after the couple exchanged their marriage vows in church. In rural Ghana, weddings include meals for the guests, prepared in takeaway boxes. In the cities, however, rich Ghanaians have a buffet for their guests.

Not surprisingly, weddings are also occasions for parents to find matches for their children and young people to meet each other, as arranged marriages are the norm. Many people have met their spouses at someone else's wedding. Males and females celebrate weddings by dancing together, drinking alcohol (depending on the religion), and good-natured socializing.

In rural Afghanistan, wedding parties are segregated by gender. The bride and her closest relatives celebrate together with other females, while the groom celebrates separately with other males, who do not see the bride during the celebration. In Islam, the term for a wedding is *nikah*. A religious figure called the "Qazi" presides over the ceremony, which consists of verses from the Quran. Only very close relatives attend, and the bride need not be present if she sends two witnesses to the formal marriage contract, but usually, only the couple is present. The custom of the bride's not being present at the wedding sometimes enables forced marriages, as others are unable to see the bride.

All Islamic weddings include standard verses from the Quran, but there are regional differences in the ceremonies and celebrations. In Afghanistan for instance, religious diversity is practically unknown, so all marriages and other domestic celebrations look much the same throughout the country, although people in urban areas tend to have a more liberal outlook. In Ghana and Côte d'Ivoire, there is more cultural diversity, distinguished along tribal lines. Brides attend the wedding, and everyone celebrates together.

When laws are not strong, some people in positions of power will take advantage of this. I have seen foreign workers in African countries having sexual affairs with Africans of various ages. Foreign men and women are often seen with younger Africans. There are many reasons for this: the Africans' hope that the foreigners would sponsor them to leave the country, another being that dating someone from a wealthy nation can sometimes be a status symbol, and yet another has to do with income inequality. This, unfortunately, gives a bad name to other, genuine couples.

Many foreigners have the financial resources to provide the local person with life's necessities. The cost of living for tourists in African countries is much less than in North America or Europe, so even middle-income tourists can enjoy a standard of living available only to wealthy Africans. Also, since laws tend to be weaker, it's much easier to exploit locals. Of course, not every affair is tainted; some romantic pairings are genuine. By and large, African women tend to be more submissive and family-oriented than women from high-income countries, so many men prefer them, thinking their partner is especially caring and trustworthy.

Another unfortunate aspect of humanity that I witnessed overseas is jealousy, which, of course, is pretty much the same everywhere, regardless of ethnicity or nationality. In Afghanistan, the conservative culture that segregates the sexes leads to jealousy and other negative feelings toward men who have more females in their personal network.

Some religious leaders who condemn co-education for girls and boys or Hollywood movies live hypocritical lives. Similarly, women who grow up in conservative religious societies also long for freedom. This sometimes finds its expression, ironically, in these women being insensitive or judgmental toward other women who travel and dress more liberally. Many Afghans have the attitude that any acceptance of cultural practices from elsewhere will erode their own culture and probably be against their religious values, so they are adamant about not accepting foreign traditions.

Ghanaian culture tends to be more liberal regarding interactions between men and women. Both work shoulder to shoulder in many occupations, including physical labor. Ghanaian women handle entire stores by themselves in rural and urban areas. This would be very unusual in Afghanistan, as most shop owners are men.

One interesting aspect of small talk that I learned in African countries was that if you tell a woman that she has gained weight or looks a little bigger, she will take it as a compliment. It's the recognition that she is eating well. Married women are meant to "fill out" as an indication that their husbands are taking good care of them. In another vein, some African women appreciate men who seem aggressive or angry, as they take those behaviors as signs of a truly manly man who is a go-getter.

Many arranged marriages in Afghanistan and most of central Asia take place within the extended family. Otherwise, the groom's family will seek out a girl who is not only from their religious sect but who also has good values and suitable education. Most important for the groom's family, however, at least in rural areas, is that the girl must be a virgin. I know of a tradition that takes place on the night after the wedding: relatives of the groom display the bridal bedsheet with its blood spots as evidence of the bride's virginity. It is shameful for the girl if the bedsheet is clean, which is taken as proof that she has had sex with a man before. To avoid this embarrassment, the newly wedded couple will sometimes paint the bedsheet with blood that they have prepared in advance.

In many Central Asian countries, local hospitals carry out "virginity tests," which are examinations of the hymens of brides-to-be. They think that such examinations are proof one way or another. In most cases, the grooms' families commission these examinations.

Some clinics also offer a surgery known as hymenoplasty, in which the hymen is manipulated in such a way that it bleeds during intercourse. Some girls have this surgery to prove they are virgins, whether they are or not. I know of instances in Tajikistan where a woman was divorced because of her inability to bleed after the wedding night.

In most countries with socially conservative traditions, sex before marriage is taboo, so these traditions of "proving" virginity remain very strong. In both Uzbekistan and Tajikistan, premarital sex is looked down upon, but in Afghanistan, when a woman is caught having sexual relations before or outside of marriage in Taliban controlled areas, they see to it that she pays for it with her life. Some filmmakers have documented this tradition and how it continues to cause much distress among women.

Foreign men should then realize that if they were to meet and date a Central Asian woman of marriageable age from a traditional and/or religious background and have sexual relations with her, and if the relationship did not work out, the woman would be hard put to marry someone of her background. The price of not being a virgin is very high for girls looking to get married; women with tarnished reputations are shunned.

The Concept of Haram

To understand the cultural choices and behaviors in Islam, it is crucial to appreciate the role of *Haram*. Haram is any action, food, or lifestyle deemed to be wrong by Islamic religious standards. An extensive behavior code is outlined in the *Quran*. No matter how well-intentioned, to do something labeled as Haram is considered a sin, and it directly or indirectly leads to harm toward yourself or others.

Telling a man or woman to do something labeled as Haram is doomed to failure due to the community backlash it will incur. A program that works for equality in Muslim-based communities will need to meticulously navigate this list of taboos to succeed.

Most low-income countries also have high fertility rates. This relates to the power of religion in these lands, where society does not encourage family planning or the use of condoms. Most people in these areas consider a child's birth to be an expression of the divine will.

Throughout my days in Fayzabad, Afghanistan, I never saw condoms for sale. Even if they were available, no one would openly acknowledge breaking the taboo against them. I never heard people talking about safe sex or condoms in Afghanistan. This strong religious and cultural bias against open discussions of sexual issues makes it extremely hard for international organizations to sponsor any development project that involves STDs or even family planning. In Afghanistan and most other predominantly Islamic countries, the use of tampons is unconsidered haram (forbidden), so they generally are not available.

Most families in Afghanistan and West Africa have four or five children who must be fed and cared for on low incomes and limited resources. This puts further pressure on the health-care and educational institutions of those lands. As a result, joblessness and the hopelessness that accompanies it leads many to crime and even terrorism. Children learn that they have a responsibility to serve their religion by increasing the number of its followers. Otherwise, they are told, they will be dominated by other religions or perish. So, religion is embedded in the culture.

In these societies, large families are a sign of good fortune and male potency. In the villages, parents with many children receive considerable respect from their peers. In Afghanistan, polygamy is legal, so families are even larger there.

Another reason for Afghanistan's high fertility rate is the practice of *nikah mut'ah*—temporary or pleasure marriage. This is a formal agreement in which the parties enter a conjugal relationship for only a specified period and can part ways when that period expires. Mut'ah is also used for sexual gratification, but many times it leads to unwanted pregnancies.

All of these factors combine with the result of many hungry and malnourished children roaming the streets. Many of the places where I worked have patriarchal societies with no government-supported social security programs. Consequently, the death of a husband and father leads to desperate circumstances for his widow(s) and their children. In some African villages, children are even sold to orphanages or sent to other cities to work, and desperate widows or divorcees find prostitution as their best option for survival. All this results from extremely unfortunate circumstances with little or no government support provided.

Homosexuality

The issue of homosexuality in African and Central Asian countries can be very fraught; in some places, even discussing the issue can be dangerous. Many people in Ghana and Côte d'Ivoire view homosexuality as a sickness imported from high-income countries. They imagine that it does not exist among the native population. People openly support the death penalty for all homosexuals.

The gender equality policies formulated in ex-soviet and other conservative countries ensure that none of their public outreach campaigns and other initiatives gives any impression that they are encouraging homosexuality in any sense. This is because many of the Central Asian countries strongly condemn homosexuality. It is a very sensitive topic that international and development organizations promoting gender equality, keep themselves at bay.

Gender roles in sub-Saharan Africa are so strong that children learn them at a very young age. Everyone must abide by them. Society accepts a strong libido in men, and adultery is also seen as normal and somewhat acceptable amongst men, but homosexuality is strictly taboo. Homosexual prostitution for foreign tourists, however, does occur, but all transactions are very discreet. If anyone with homosexual tendencies visits sub-Saharan Africa, I strongly advise them to keep those tendencies confidential.

In Afghanistan, homosexuality and cross-dressing are widely seen as indecent activities, owing to traditional Islamic views on appropriate gender roles and sexual conduct. The Taliban executes homosexuals in public. During my years in Afghanistan, I never heard homosexuality being discussed seriously; it was as if the tendency or practice did not exist. I did hear jokes about it, and I saw the absolute fear that people had of even expressing any tolerance for homosexuality.

Of course, just because it's taboo does not mean it does not exist. It is still highly prevalent in Afghanistan. Since the country is very conservative, a man has no casual access to girls and women except in the hidden brothels in Kabul. Because of this, in rural areas, there is a form of child sexual abuse between older men and young adolescent males; it is known as *bacha bazi*, which means "boy play." The young men who get caught up in this practice are known as dancing boys. Given how conservative the society is, militia members also do not have easy access to women, so they sometimes kidnap boys to humiliate and rape. Other boys become prostitutes for adult men, regardless of their sexual orientation.

This practice is so common that many Afghan families fear their young boys being kidnapped for bacha bazi. Boys as young as seven years old become victims of this crime; by the time young men are 17 or 18, they no longer attract this sort of attention. In some cases, revenge kidnappings have occurred as an eye-for-an-eye reaction.

Bacha bazi still occurs in most provinces of Afghanistan. Teenage boys are forced to dress in women's clothing, participate in dance competitions, and engage in sexual acts with older men. Most Afghans are against this practice, but few speak up against it because of fear of the militias and tribal leaders responsible for the prevalence of the practice.

Sexuality is a taboo subject in Afghanistan. Consequently, sexual crimes against minors and women are pervasive. No male colleague ever spoke to me about finding an Afghan woman attractive, but I frequently heard my male colleagues speak about the appearance of foreign female colleagues, which is much more acceptable.

As a foreigner in the country, I was sometimes approached by Afghan gay men who would try to test my sexuality. It's safer for them to approach foreign men than another Afghan man. Some try to chat with you under a different name on Facebook or some other online messaging system to learn your thoughts about homosexuality. Of course, they do this to find a partner. Even foreign gay men sometimes drop hints in text messages to see your reaction. I believe that this is a direct result of Afghans' extremely conservative attitudes towards sex. Unfortunately, all Afghan men and women are supposed to publicly condemn homosexuality, even though some identify with various sexual orientations. To express their culturally unacceptable sexuality, they must leave the country.

Afghan and African families who know their sons or daughters identify as homosexuals still force them to marry someone of the opposite sex, giving in to societal pressure. An unfortunately high percentage of these parents believe that marriage will "turn" their child heterosexual. Since the culture forbids premarital sex, the partner does not know that their new partner is not interested in having a physical relationship with them until marriage. During this process, by conforming to social norms they end up affecting the life of their spouse as well. As divorces are uncommon and stigmatized. This is a similar practice seen in many south Asian countries where homosexuality is frowned upon.

Many people who identify with non-heterosexuality in conservative areas of Asia and Africa seek marriage partners of the opposite sex that also identify as such. That way, the rest of the world acknowledges that they are a married couple. But in their private and hidden life, they often have other relations.

Usually, when I went as a young solo traveler to countries like Uzbekistan, Tajikistan, and some West African nations, I was offered prostitutes by the hotel managers or taxi drivers. They seem to hold a perception that solo travelers are in their country for sexual pleasure, including sex tourism, rather than cultural tourism. Not many females travel solo in these communities because they tend to marry early and do not get a chance to travel alone. Most have to travel with their husbands and children, so the sight of Western women traveling solo is quite startling.

A young male traveler heading for these countries should be prepared for questioning at the immigration control centers. Simultaneously, he should be prepared to receive offers for prostitutes from hotel managers or taxi drivers.

Culturally in Asian and African contexts, people are more open when it comes to speaking about their personal and family lives. They often ask one another questions that would be considered "too personal" in other parts of the world. For instance, they might ask,

"When are you getting married?" or "When are you planning to have kids?" and these questions would cause no offense. They do not mean to pry into others' private lives; they just do not consider such questions personal. Besides, their culture demands that people get married by a certain point in their lives.

Chapter 4.

Gender Roles

Industrialization and feminist movements have allowed women in high-income countries to take on unconventional roles not often seen in other parts of the world. For example, they can work outside the home, own land, vote, and live without a spouse or male relative. It is easy to forget that this is not a universal custom, even in this era.

Gender roles and responsibilities vary widely throughout the world. In traditional households of low-income countries, women are expected to be homemakers, caregivers, and mothers to their children. They are expected to be good cooks and maintain the household, and men are expected to go out and earn a livelihood. This is as normal in low-income countries as feminine independence is in other countries.

Men, especially in ex-soviet countries of Uzbekistan and Tajikistan, are meant and tend to be more physically aggressive and strong; any demonstration of soft emotions can be seen as unmanly. He should always be the breadwinner and only be involved with what is considered manly hobbies. He is responsible for all outside chores that demand physical strength.

On the other hand, a woman should always take care of her physical self, wear feminine dresses, and should always be the one to do household chores. She should love and want kids and take full responsibility for the care of children when they arrive. These gender roles might be changing or becoming less assertive, but that was my impression at the time.

In both Afghanistan and sub-Saharan Africa, I noticed a single common factor among all the women I met. Every one of them prioritized their families before their personal needs. They all wanted bright futures for their children and respected names in the community for their families. They would even sacrifice their own happiness to achieve this, a notion that is unconventional in developed nations.

Undoubtedly, Afghans are among the most hospitable, soft-spoken, warm, and friendly people I have ever encountered. But there is a generally held belief that many differences exist between men and women. As a result, there are very different cultural expectations for both men and women. They expect women to behave in specific ways and obey certain rules without question. Women's behavior is under constant scrutiny. Any attempt to violate this system is considered an offense to their culture and is not taken lightly.

Despite this general perspective, many Afghan men admit that women are not being given the best treatment. They agree that there must be some changes to the system. However, radical change will not come easily. Their hesitation is mostly due to the cultural repercussions and armed conflicts that might ensue. The changes are not feasible unless community leaders, religious leaders, and top-level politicians strongly advocate for them.

Once they are married, many Afghan women focus on having and raising children. Even working mothers are still mostly responsible for taking care of their children. As a result, Afghan society looks down on feminist movements imported from high-income countries. They fear that the beliefs and attitudes taught by modern feminism will cause women to walk away from their motherly responsibilities to pursue career ambitions.

The ideas touted by many feminists, such as zero tolerance for any kind of abuse and an easy road to divorce, do not play well in war-torn and low-income countries. Women in those places do not have the liberty to speak up and file for divorce.

In Afghanistan, divorce is an embarrassment for all concerned: men, women, and their families. The stigma can be so strong that it even affects the chances of arranged marriage for the divorced couples' siblings.

To complicate matters further, the community often stigmatizes divorced men even more than they do women. Divorced men are seen as less manly and incompetent at managing their households and relationships with their women. The pressure to avoid being labeled in this manner can lead to dangerous conditions for the woman. For example, some men may inflict severe mental and physical abuse on their spouse to keep her too fearful or dependent on them to consider divorce. We see this tactic in even the most developed countries. Afghan women subjected to this kind of abuse do not have the opportunities and resources to safely leave such environments.

Another factor is the unfortunately low literacy rate among women in low-income countries. According to the World Bank, Afghanistan's literacy rate among women is only about 30 percent. As a result, it is challenging for unmarried and divorced women to find decent jobs and make a living on their own. Women simply cannot afford to divorce their husbands, even if the opportunity is there, especially if the cost of living includes caring for children.

Many international development programs are short-sighted. They manage to achieve a certain gender ratio or reach a target number of women in their literacy programs. But if these programs fail to instill a basic understanding that men and women have equal capabilities, the women draw no long-term benefit from them. Knowledge with no direction does nothing for the problem in the end.

In my experience, international agencies should tailor their gender-equality programs to the country and culture they want to reach. This tailoring should include consideration of the religious and ethnic context of the area. If they did this, the movement for equality could be implemented in the most effective ways for that region.

The Gender Double Standard

Another thing I noticed is that Afghan men closely observe and judge the behavior of Afghan women both within and outside the country, regardless of the relationship between them.

Once puberty hits, women are supposed to guard themselves against any form of improper behavior with men. This is taken to such an extreme that they are not even allowed to talk or interact with the opposite sex without a male guardian present. Young girls are allowed to enjoy themselves at public parks, using the swings and playing with the boys, but once puberty arrives, only males can openly enjoy such pleasures.

While I was in Afghanistan, whenever I entered a shop or handicraft exhibition that had a female attendant, I always saw an adult Afghan male guardian nearby. These men listen to the customer-attendant conversations for any indication that the talk is not focused on the product or deal. Flirting between female attendants and their male customers is strictly forbidden, even if the customer is only speaking lightheartedly.

The opinions of Afghan men in this regard can have considerable influence, regardless of whether the women under discussion are related to them or not. Their opinions can even reach across borders to influence the women's social circles there.

I heard of an Afghan girl who went to Tajikistan to study for a month. One day, she exchanged her traditional garb for a skirt like other Tajik girls. Her male colleagues reported this to the people back in their village. When she came home, the community embarrassed not only her but her parents as well. This was no small thing for her and her family. Once a girl gets a bad name in her community, she will have considerable difficulty finding a suitable marriage partner. Few men want to be paired with a woman with a bad reputation.

There is a considerable double standard, however. Afghan men may temporarily tarnish their reputations when they are in foreign countries by visiting prostitutes, frequenting night clubs, or consuming alcohol, but when they return to Afghanistan, their good names are restored. The culture ultimately tolerates that sort of behavior in men, but Afghan women must always behave modestly.

Most Afghan men forbid their female relatives or female colleagues from traveling to other countries apart from Pakistan. In general, they express concern that exposure to foreign cultures will corrupt the women. In my field visits to Tajikistan, there were never any female Afghan colleagues. Usually, the only women who traveled with Afghan men were foreign workers.

No Photographs

During my field visits for women entrepreneur programs, I always had to get a woman's consent to take her picture. Not just her consent but also that of her male Afghan guardians. Women are very fearful of having their pictures taken or shared due to the long list of things viewed as inappropriate or Haram in their culture. I know of a video that showed two women clapping while men were dancing at a social gathering. This video went viral, and eventually, several individuals murdered the women out of religious fury.

Afghan families typically forbid their female members from posting any pictures of themselves on social media, and most female Afghan professionals are hesitant to have meetings via webcam. Posting pictures online would tarnish the family's good name and, as seen with the unfortunate girls in the video, could incur threats to their lives as well.

My advice is to never snap or post a picture of an Afghan woman without her consent. It can be dangerous for her, depending on the philosophies and perspectives of her family.

The Segregation of Men and Women

In the conservative Afghan society, men and women are segregated during celebrations. Women dance only in the company of other women or close family members. In some rural communities, men even consider music and dance as Haram.

Afghans generally believe that dancing is a sensual act for women. As a result, it should not be done in front of men who are not immediate family members.

When Afghan women do work outside the house, they are expected to maintain their modesty at all times. This means, for example, that women are not allowed to have romantic relationships in the workplace. Typically, such activity, whether consensual or not, even if it is unwanted sexual harassment, is viewed as the fault of the woman. Therefore, if there are rumors that the woman has comported herself in an inappropriate manner, she will be dismissed or transferred to another department.

Many Afghans marry within the family—first, second, and third cousins. This makes reporting the abuse much more difficult because Afghan society is extremely conservative. This is especially so in rural areas where sex segregation starts at an early age.

As a consequence to Afghanistan's patriarchal society, economic dependency on men and social stigma put parents in a difficult spot. Daughters can often be considered as a burden, while a son will earn money, carry on the family legacy, inherit the father's property and stay home to care for their aging parents. So, all families desire to have a son and families without boys are subject to pity and contempt.

To counter this, some reassign their daughter's gender at birth in a practice known as "bacha posh." A cultural practice called "bacha posh" encourages parents to dress their daughters as sons for a better future. The term "Bacha Posh" means a "girl dressed like a boy in the local Dari language. This enables the child to behave more freely; wherein one can attend school, escort her sisters in public, and work outside the home. She is treated as such, although family members, close friends, and health and education officials are usually aware of the truth. The child can then obtain a better education, go out independently, and act as a chaperone to her sisters. Also, it assists her in carrying out the duties of a son without getting harassed.

Significantly, this practice allows the family to avoid the social stigma associated with not having any male children. A girl living as a boy will dress in characteristic male clothing, have her hair cut short, and use a male name. Bacha Posh is a struggle for a little freedom of girls in a highly patriarchal society. It usually ends when the girl reaches puberty.

The Role of the Mahram

As Afghanistan is a very patriarchal society, a woman must have a *mahram*—a male or female escort who is a family member—accompany her whenever she leaves the house for more than three days. This is to prevent men from accosting her and to assure her modesty and sexual purity. Sometimes, a woman's grandmother serves as the mahram, but this is ironic because an older woman can be more vulnerable to health and personal security concerns.

The custom can become an obstacle during training and conferences in other cities, as travel budgets are limited and paying for two people to travel costs considerably more than for one. Consequently, women have fewer opportunities to attend conferences and meetings in locations away from their homes.

Even if a mahram accompanies a group of very well-educated women, they must still obey him or her during their travels. The mahram keeps a constant check to ensure the women are not talking to men, do not go anywhere that might dishonor them, or do anything against their religious and moral codes. If a woman disobeys her mahram, her family and employer will hear about it, and her reputation and career could suffer.

The Reasoning Behind these Restrictions

In rural areas, most Afghan men imagine foreign cultures as evil influences that could pollute the minds of their youth and women. So even when Afghan women have the opportunity to travel to lands that have a liberal lifestyle, such as Tajikistan, Uzbekistan, India, or Dubai, the men hesitate to allow them to go, even with a mahram.

When asked why they restrict the lives of Afghan women, Afghan men say that their customs protect the women or that they don't want Afghan women to adopt foreign ideas such as western feminism—

which often portrays things considered Haram in their religion, such as talking back to a husband or freedom of sexual exploration.

Even though Afghanistan and Tajikistan have a similar language and religion, the lifestyles of Afghan and Tajik women tend to be very different. Because of the Russian/Soviet influence in Tajikistan and Uzbekistan, women are encouraged to be more independent, become educated, and follow their passions.

Married Women and Culture

Afghan men always show great respect to their colleagues' wives and mothers, but unattached women are subject to all sorts of sexual harassment. Most Afghan men also see single women "of a certain age" or divorced women as morally inferior. However, they treat married women with respect. If the object of derogatory behavior is later found to be the wife of a respectable man in the community, she will immediately receive all due respect. The respect a woman receives depends on her marital status, who her spouse is, how her husband respects her, and the situation of her children.

After the birth of a colleague's child, a typical Afghan man will respectfully ask about the health of the newborn but hesitate to ask about the health of the new mother. Few men ever see or meet their colleagues' wives. Young women seldom remain single for long, so society does not question their morality as they age.

In high-income countries, individuals on the "dating market" have different values. In other words, men between the ages of 25 and 45 are considered most desirable, while the comparable age range for women is about 20 to 32. The general idea applies in Afghanistan too, but the ideal age range for women to get married is between 16 and 25. Well-educated women are sometimes regarded as arrogant or rebellious, so some families in rural Afghanistan also prefer less-educated women for brides. They are considered more submissive and better homemakers.

Land Ownership and Work Opportunities

Afghan law is clear that men and women enjoy equal property rights under the country's 2004 constitution. Unfortunately, the reality is far from what the law prescribes. A combination of tradition and common law keeps most Afghan women unaware of their right to own land and other property. In this patriarchal society, the cultural expectation is that a woman's husband will be her economic provider, so she does not need her land in her name.

Those expectations extend to preventing women from inheriting land from their fathers, who bequeath it instead to their sons. The sons will, in turn, use the land to provide for their own families, not those of their sisters.

This cultural thinking does not just result in women having no share of their father's land. It also puts an obligation on them to be good, traditional wives. Furthermore, it hampers women's entrepreneurship, as they have no land to act as collateral to grow their businesses. This is no small matter. According to the 2017 report from the Council on Foreign Relations, if Afghan women could, in fact, own land, agricultural production rates could increase by 20 to 30 percent. This would significantly contribute to improved food security throughout the country.

And finally, land ownership by women correlates with reduced violence against them. Almost nine out of ten Afghan women face physical, sexual, or psychological violence, and just as many are forced into marriage. With economic empowerment, many women could escape these abusive relationships.

In Tajikistan, many women work in construction or public places. They have much better lives and more freedom than women in Afghanistan, but Tajikistan, unfortunately, presents other social issues. As of 2020, about one-third of the men in Tajikistan and Uzbekistan have emigrated to Russia for work. One reason is that many of the former Soviet republics have pacts with Russia that allows their citizens to work in Russia without having to overcome onerous bureaucratic hurdles. This has led to an unbalanced sex ratio in Tajikistan, as many men who work abroad divorce their Tajik wives and end up marrying foreign women.

Many of these Tajik women learn of their divorce by a text message, as Tajikistan is among the few Muslim nations where men can divorce their wives by repeating the word *taloq* (divorce) three times. They can do it face to face, over the phone, or simply by sending a text.

Unfortunately, Tajik culture always considers divorce the fault of the woman, so few divorced women ever receive child support or alimony. Hence, many children of divorced women start working at a young age to sustain their households, and their education suffers as a consequence.

In Afghanistan, I observed that conservative traditions hamper women's careers in other ways, such as their ability to take on leadership roles. None of my male colleagues would ever call or otherwise contact any of our local Afghan female colleagues after office hours. Traditional Afghan families do not appreciate having their daughters or daughters-in-law contacted in the evening, especially when the call comes from a male co-worker.

This is not a simple matter for a female leader. The tenuous security situation in Afghanistan and other conflict zones requires all organization heads and regional representatives to be available by phone at any time of the day or night. Their responsibilities might also require them to travel in the late evening or early morning in response to an emergency. For instance, when Taliban landmines killed several of our colleagues, swift communication and travel preparations were essential. Our regional representative had to be contacted immediately (around midnight) to begin making arrangements for travel to the district for the funerals. Had the representative been a woman, she probably would not have had the flexibility to respond as quickly as necessary. Since the responsibility for taking care of children falls mostly on women, leaving the children at home while traveling for field visits may meet resistance from their families. Also, most women do not travel without a mahram, so this adds another barrier to their attaining higher positions. As most of the upper-level managers must travel frequently. Furthermore, respect in Afghanistan correlates with age, so few men would accept a younger woman as their boss and administrator.

Another factor, in both Afghanistan and Ghana, is pregnancy. Both of these countries have very high fertility rates. One of the most common wedding gifts in Central Asia is diapers, an indication that marriages are meant to produce children. Having children is an integral part of all families in Afghanistan and sub-Saharan Africa. In all my experience in field missions, I never met a family that willingly decided to have no children. Because of these cultural expectations, all employers assume that all young female hires will eventually become pregnant and take time off for maternity leave, which limits women's potential for management positions. That is why most of the successful women in Afghanistan are either elderly or come from very affluent or famous families. Those conditions give them a platform that common women don't have.

I recall a workshop in Fayzabad. An officer was touting the achievements in his district and commended his new female intern by stating, "She is so good she is almost like a man." I remember the room bursting into laughter, while the foreign female workers in the room looked absolutely flabbergasted. Any employee saying the same in North America or Western Europe could easily lose their job or jeopardize their reputation, but in Afghanistan, this was seen through a different lens. To the officer, it was merely a mark of humorous high praise for her ability.

Female Circumcision

During my time in Ghana assisting the Health Directorate, I realized that the practice of female genital mutilation was still prevalent even though the Ghana Health Directorate had introduced several programs to increase awareness about the dangers of this custom. Female genital mutilation (FGM), also known as female circumcision, is the ritual cutting or removal of some or all the external female genitalia. This can very negatively affect a woman's health later in life.

Substantial number of men are in favor of female circumcision, believing that it dampens or altogether removes the pleasure women experience during sex. In their view, it reduces whatever incentive a woman might have for adultery. Many also cite religion as a factor in their support of the practice. Unfortunately, FGM contributes to high maternal mortality rates in any country where it is prevalent.

Cultural Perceptions

In Afghanistan, all women mostly wear a full burqa in public. Men would stare in shock at any woman who revealed more than her eyes, hands, and feet. In Ghana, however, the situation is on the flip side. A lot of Ghanaian women openly breastfeed their babies. Sometimes, they work bare-breasted in the fields, and no one considers their state of undress out of the ordinary. In most of sub-Saharan Africa, breasts have not been sexualized, and bare breasts are part of the traditional tribal dress worn on ceremonial or celebratory occasions.

Despite being fully covered, Afghan women suffer violence and abuse at a significantly higher rate than what is observed in most other countries of the world. That should make us realize that many crimes against women do not occur because of how they dress.

Chapter 5.

Discrimination Factors

Discrimination is very common all around the world. Whether it's gender, age, religion, ethnic background, caste, etc., humans tend to divide themselves into the in-group and out-group; Us Vs. Them. The "other" could be the ethnic Hazara group in Afghanistan, people of African ancestry in China, or even migrants from Alabama in New York. People all around the world have been on either side of discrimination, directly or indirectly, intentionally or unintentionally. Our everyday behaviors can sometimes reveal preconceived notions that we might not even be aware of.

Before my development missions, most of my thinking about people and culture was based on what I saw in the media, especially movies. The entertainment industry usually depicted African-Americans in a negative light, mostly in criminal roles. Muslims were usually portrayed similarly as terrorists, especially after all the terrorist attacks in recent decades. If I had never been exposed to people of backgrounds different from my own through my travels and global living, I probably would still have those notions.

During my global living, I always tried to immerse myself in the local culture by learning the language and customs of the people I happened to find myself among. However, I would still find myself (frustratingly) unconsciously reflecting on various incidents through a racist or religiously biased lens. I also observed a lot of racism towards certain communities around the world, especially in conflict situations.

In Afghanistan, for example, I found that a person's ethnic or religious background was a noteworthy definer of who they were. In the country, if you belong to the Hazara ethnic community or a religious minority, you face a lot of discrimination in every aspect of life.

I made similar observations in rural areas of Ghana and Côte d'Ivoire, where an employer's ethnic or tribal identity almost always carries through the entire payroll of the company' even the business owner's driver and domestic help would be of the same tribe. To make it worse and more identifiable, many people bear specific kinds of scars on their faces that identify them as members of a certain tribe. These scars are inflicted on very young children and mark a person for life, and anyone who is familiar with this system and practice can ascertain their tribal background just by looking at them.

In Afghanistan, one's manner of dress is way more important than in other countries. Many people will treat you with respect if you dress in the local attire and observe the sexual segregation of society. The length of a man's beard is also a way to determine who is an outsider and who is not.

In fact, people make all kinds of assumptions about one's identity based on beard length. Elderly men typically have very long beards, which reflect their strong religious beliefs. A long beard could also signify that one is a Hajji—a Muslim who has completed the Hajj (pilgrimage) to Makkah. So, men who have beards (and especially long beards) receive a lot of respect, even though it may be unconscious.

In Afghanistan, one's name can mark one as an outsider, even if one is a native Afghan. A person with an Islamic name will receive more respect from the local population than someone with a name that has no Islamic connotations. This applies even to devout Muslims who bear names common in non-Islamic countries. For people from high-income countries, name discrimination is much more rampant in Afghanistan than in Ghana or Côte d'Ivoire. One reason for this is that African countries have a significant Christian population. People there are more acquainted with others who have names taken from the Bible and still treat them respectfully. In Afghanistan, however, almost the entire population has Islamic names, and individuals from the very small religious minority that do not have such names are marginalized.

I personally experienced this at Kabul airport. The attitude of security officials there changed when they realized that I had a non-Islamic name. Before that, the texture of my hair, my skin tone, beard and the traditional Afghani attire I was wearing allowed me to blend in. I receive a normal level of respect, but after they learned my name, some of these guards became much less friendly, and I had to go through more intense security clearance at the airport. I felt this as a kind of retaliation against the United States (U.S.) and other high-income countries, racially profiling Afghans or people with Islamic names at their airports.

This treatment reminded me of the months immediately following the terrorist attacks of 9-11. During that time, I went through similarly intense scrutiny when traveling through U.S. airports. Other people who have a darker skin tone and/or an Arabic- or Islamic-sounding name have also told me about how they were harassed and maltreated at U.S. airports back then. Perhaps a word of that discrimination in the United States got back to Afghanistan and led to this practice of security officials in Kabul treating citizens of non-Islamic countries with more security protocols.

I personally felt that Afghan people were very visual in terms of treating people. If you have brown skin, they always assume that you come from Arab or South Asia countries. Because of that, many minorities from Europe and the Americas who work in Afghanistan struggle to justify their ethnic origin. To most Afghans, an American or European is always of Caucasian origin, although this thinking is changing in some Afghan cities.

You can see this bias also in the greater credibility that Afghans attribute to Americans or Europeans of Arab and Afghan descent when these foreigners speak in public, implement policies, or make field visits. Afghans see these Arab foreigners as their own people, much like North Americans view Europeans. It seems as though we naturally accept and trust people who look like us. We tend to feel safer and more comfortable when approached by someone with a similar ethnic background or accent. No surprise, then, that Afghans also feel safer when interacting with people who at least look like they comprehend their culture and religion. Even though one's skin color should not be a factor in making assumptions about another person; unfortunately, the world is not there yet.

After Barack Obama was elected President of the United States, many public places in Ghana and Côte d'Ivoire displayed small U.S. flags next to those of their own country. People felt as though one of their own had been elected to the most powerful position in the world. Celebrations occurred all across Africa. Taxis, buses, shops, and some people's houses also displayed pictures of Barack Obama. Children were named after him. Obama's presidency led many Africans to regain some of their trust in the United States as a land of equal opportunity.

Overall, the treatment that the United States shows to African countries is a good indicator of how Africans perceive the United States and its presence on the African continent. Recently, however, deadly attacks by U.S. police on African Americans have tarnished the reputation of the United States as a country that respects its diversity.

Decades of war have brought numerous peoples to Afghanistan, such as Americans, British, Russians, Kazakhs, Tajiks, Pakistanis, etc. For their part, many Afghans left their country as refugees to Iran; many emigrated to Pakistan and some to India. In all of Central and South Asia, no country has taken in more refugees than Pakistan. Pakistan has played a very crucial and helpful role in Afghanistan during the conflicts.

India has also provided much aid to Afghanistan and hosts medical tourists from Afghanistan for very affordable rates. Both countries have assisted the Afghans in many ways throughout their conflicts. Some argue that Pakistan has done more than India, and some argue otherwise. From the Afghan perspective, Iran has discriminated against them. Many Afghans in Tehran experience strong prejudice towards them. Often, this takes the form of being unable to rent a home, as many Iranian landlords do not trust Afghans and other hardships that come with being a refugee.

During my field trips, I met the occasional Afghan of Russian or Kazakh origin, people whose fathers had come to Afghanistan as soldiers, decided to stay, and raised families in Afghanistan. With Afghan wives, they could not transfer their language skills to their children. So now, some of these offspring have claimed citizenship in Kazakhstan or Russia by ancestry and moved to those countries to escape the war. But they often and unfortunately experience discrimination against them in their ancestral countries. Even though they are citizens of their fathers' countries, they still are perceived as refugees.

In China, one of the most common types of racism towards foreigners becomes evident when foreigners apply for jobs to teach English. In the past few decades, China has raised most of its population above the poverty line. It also significantly expanded its manufacturing industry and now exports many goods around the world.

Its factories manufacture goods that are much cheaper to buy than similar goods manufactured elsewhere. With this expansion, China has welcomed increasing numbers of foreign traders and businesses into the country in the last few years. Foreign tourism, manufacturing, and trade have combined in China to provide economic prosperity for the resident population. Many signs and labels in China are now printed in English, making the country more friendly and comfortable for foreigners.

With all the economic expansion, China's demand for foreign English teachers in private and public schools and private tutors has grown exponentially. Prosperous Chinese families seem to prefer foreign English teachers for their children. These families contact private institutions that can arrange a teacher for them. Big schools and institutes hire these foreign English teachers directly from North America, the UK, or Australia, but many also hire foreigners who already live in China.

During my stay in China, I observed that the hiring process involved creating photo albums of available teachers. Parents or the students themselves choose their teachers from those albums, and in the mind of many Chinese people, a native English speaker is always Caucasian. Consequently, they usually choose a Caucasian teacher.

This, unfortunately, means that many African-American, Asian-American or other non-Caucasian English teachers do not get hired or face difficulties in China, even though they may be native English speakers with perfect native accents. It also means that English teachers from Eastern Europe and Russia get hired even though their English might be subpar. This kind of bias for Caucasian English teachers is very common all around China, but most Chinese do not consider this as a form of discrimination. Even online classified advertisements like you would find on Kijiji, or Craigslist often mentions that they have vacancies for English teachers who are of the Caucasian race. And if that bias does not appear explicitly, the pictures required for an application serve as a racial screen for these jobs.

Travel

Many have noted that Afghanistan passports have many problems. These passports allow their holders to travel to other countries, and, depending on the passport, you may or may not also require visas to visit those countries. Passports from high-income countries, on the other hand, give travelers the liberty to travel to many countries without needing a visa or prior travel arrangements.

Afghan passports allow their holder's visa-free access to only a handful of countries. So Afghan citizens must apply for a visa to visit almost any other country. The situation is to a great extent the same for citizens of Côte d'Ivoire and Ghana; they also must have a visa to visit almost any other country. In these countries, the process of seeking a visa can be costly, lengthy, and complicated, and obtaining a visa for a Western European or North American county can be even more so.

For instance, when Afghans plan to attend conferences in the United States, they must complete several forms concerning their personal and family histories, their financial situation, and their personal ties in Afghanistan. They must also undergo medical checkups, which could involve travel to cities distant from their homes, and provide security clearances from other countries they have visited. Most also must go through an interview at the embassy of the country they intend to visit. This is all to prove that they would not overstay in the country illegally and that their intentions are legitimate.

Sometimes, appointments at embassies in Afghanistan must be scheduled six months in advance. Throughout my time in Afghanistan and sub-Saharan Africa, I saw the visa applications of many of my colleagues rejected, even though they had strong intentions of coming back to the country. The fees for visas can also be very expensive—$500 to $1,000 in some cases—and these fees are usually non-refundable if the embassy rejects the application. For many unmarried male citizens of low-income countries, the chances of getting a visa are very bleak.

This further disadvantages many professionals from low-income countries who are looking to work for international organizations. Such organizations usually prioritize their recruiting efforts with the citizenship of the applicant in mind. They know that the visa processes for citizens of low-income countries can be gruesome and expensive, hampering their availability for international travel.

Unfortunately, even the immigration and customs officials in some countries treat travelers differently depending on the origin of the passports they hold. While traveling with Afghans, I have seen many of them questioned more rigorously than travelers from other nations. For example, every time I traveled to Tajikistan with Afghan colleagues, the Tajik authorities were very strict with the Afghans.

Some officials even ask very personal and disrespectful questions about people's private lives. Similarly, immigration officers can quite often be very rude to citizens of sub-Saharan countries as well.

Recruitment

My perception of the recruitment process is that all international organizations somewhat bias their policies for recruiting professional expatriates toward citizens of high-income countries. This could be a reflection of the fact that high-income countries fund almost all high-level UN positions. People in power tend to fill open positions with individuals from their own or other high-income countries.

Many organizations typically prefer people from Western Europe or North America. Still, there is a general perception out there that applicants from those countries are more qualified. Filling such positions generally takes a long time, sometimes even up to a year.

Such organizations also prefer to staff their offices and other operations in low-income countries with locals who have studied in Europe or North America. Many people from low-income countries regard academic degrees from their national universities with less respect than those from universities in the high-income countries, although degrees from the few prestigious and transparently run universities in certain low-income countries do command high respect.

In Uzbekistan, all my work colleagues had some certification or degree from a university in a high-income country. In general, local universities were considered to have low standards where many students committed plagiarism. So overall, employers openly gave preference to individuals with foreign credentials.

Many international organizations and donor agencies also discriminate after hiring processes based on the citizenship of the applicant. This sort of discrimination can even extend beyond hiring.

People from high-income countries often receive higher starting salaries, and once they begin working, they get more and better salary raises compared to their colleagues from low-income countries, even if they have the same job responsibilities.

Throughout the international development world, the networks of Western Europeans and North Americans seem much closer, more effective, and more involved in decision making. Even international governments and donor agencies seem to have more trust in and are willing to donate to organizations largely staffed by North Americans and Western Europeans. It's somehow considered that they have more credibility and a better work ethic, which may or may not always be true. This puts other local organizations solely run by the locals that can't afford to hire International staff at a disadvantage.

I have seen that most locals in low-income countries tend to respect foreign workers from high-income countries than those from other nations. A perception seems to exist that individuals from low-income countries work in international development because of the relatively good salaries they can earn, but that individuals from high-income countries do this kind of work out of humanitarian or altruistic motives. So, one's country of origin can have a lot of influence on getting hired, getting a good salary and good raises, and serving in positions of authority, and just overall respect.

Fig. 11 Picture of Barack Obama on a bag in Ghana. Many named their baby boy "Barack" after his win in 2008 elections, but as time has gone on, fewer people want to name their kid after the former president.

Fig. 12 Typical Street in Kabul, Afghanistan

Chapter 6.

The Importance of Religion

Religion is significant, especially for those living in conflict zones. Most people in developing and conflict countries practice one religion or another, and it's the anchor for the principles and values of millions. Religion, by its very nature, has the power to give people more peace of mind and a respite from everyday struggles. People often pray more during hard times than when everything is fine, so living with war, conflict, and/or danger poses such significant stress that they may very well find themselves praying more often than they would otherwise.

The religion of Islam has a powerful impact on the Afghan people, many of whom appear to live for the religion. In my view, desperation is one of the main reasons for this, as many long for the support that comes with being a part of a religious community. Islam is an entire way of life, so perhaps it is no surprise that individuals born into this environment where religion has such strong importance and meaning would follow their religion so zealously.

A common religion creates many social ties. During my time in Western Africa, I frequently saw the more tremendous respect people offered to those who shared their religious beliefs, be they Christian or Muslim. This is not to say that disrespect was shown to individuals who were not of like religion, but in contrast, with individuals from outside their religious circle, they'll generally preach to and try to convert individuals from outside their own circles to their particular religion.

In Afghanistan, in particular, this phenomenon is powerful. Discounting the Taliban, who kill people belonging to other religions or sects, Afghans typically keep a distance from individuals who profess other religions. The country defines itself as an Islamic republic, and only a few religious minorities can survive within its borders.

Marriages outside one's sect are rare. If an Afghan Muslim wants to marry a non-Muslim, the marriage takes place only after the non-Muslim partner formally converts to Islam. The holy book—the Quran—has the final say, and no one may challenge it.

Education

Many elderly people in rural Afghanistan were educated in Islamic religious schools called *madrassas* (mosque schools), which are still common in Afghanistan. Primarily, these schools teach the Quran and some aspects of calculation, grammar, poetry, history, etc. Unfortunately, however, the education one receives in a madrassa rarely provides the student with the skills necessary for modern-day, technology savvy, well-paid jobs. Religious schools focus mainly on lessons from the holy book; subjects such as science, math, and other secular subjects are not taught as a priority because religious teachings are the primary concern.

Of course, not all madrassas are the same, although most emphasize rote learning over critical thinking. In madrassas, students learn about religious values with the expectation that they will accept them as given and without offering any challenge to their authority. The precise curriculum of Islamic religious schools varies from country to country, but overall, they emphasize Islam over just about everything else. For example, the interpretation of Islam taught in conservative rural areas of Afghanistan is distinct from the madrassa education taught in Côte d'Ivoire or Turkey.

Many older individuals in rural Afghanistan prefer to educate their youth in madrassas versus regular schools in part because these institutions are part of their cultural identity. In general, they look down on secular education common in Europe and North America. Perhaps this is the result of having been invaded by other countries so many times over a vast number of years. In the face of those threats, cultures have learned to hang on to traditional cultural and religious beliefs as a way of defending themselves from the influence of foreign powers.

Honor Killing

Honor killing is a phenomenon that is still very much in practice in Afghanistan and Pakistan. Its victims include anyone who brings shame to the family, and the action is carried out by a member or members of the victim's family. Society may be overly restrictive for women, who must usually follow a different standard of behavior than men.

For example, if a young woman falls in love with a young man with whom her parents don't approve of, both the young woman and her lover may be murdered. There are occasions when vengeance for such dishonor is not accomplished through outright murder; it could also come via an acid attack or through severe physical abuse. The loss of a family's honor is a grave matter in rural areas of Afghanistan and Pakistan. For those who share this mindset, a family's honor must be maintained even at the cost of family members' lives.

This aspect of honor is another reason why young women are married off even before they finish high school. Many families' leaders believe their young women will be corrupted if they are without a male guardian. As I mentioned earlier, there was a famous case with a video of some young women innocently clapping and singing while boys were dancing at a social gathering. The video went viral, and all of the people in the video were murdered—as hard as it may be for those of other cultures to understand, these murders were considered honor killings.

Society can be overly restrictive for women, who are often forced to follow a different standard of behavior than men. This case was just one of the thousands that have occurred in Afghanistan over the years. Unfortunately, many incidents involving honor killings are not even reported due to the shame that doing so would cause a family.

Sometimes, people have killed their own daughters or sisters to protect their honor. Whether a woman is raped or not, families tend to believe she is at fault, and the best way to protect the family's honor is to murder her. Naturally, many Afghans find the matter of honor killings gruesome, to say the least, and would like to see things change. But those people are generally in the minority or have lesser political authority. Speaking out about changing the culture in this way may result in their murder or a severe beating.

Even a false accusation of blasphemy can result in a murder, especially when a mob gathers over the accusation. There have been instances when minorities are also blackmailed. For example, if one owes money to someone of a minority religion, that person may accuse the minority of blasphemy, so they don't have to pay. Someone can also accuse another of blasphemy if they dislike them or have a personal disagreement against them. Instances like these have later resulted in prosecution or even murder by an angry mob.

Blasphemy

Blasphemy is an extremely sensitive subject in Afghanistan. When satirical French weekly magazine *Charlie Hebdo* published cartoons of the Prophet in 2011 and 2015, massive protests erupted in Afghanistan, which lasted for many days. Leaders in the Islamic world consider such acts as publishing cartoons of the Prophet to be blasphemy, and incidents such as these may severely jeopardize the lives of non-Muslims living in Afghanistan.

Retaliation from Afghan religious groups puts all foreigners and NATO troops in danger. Similarly, any public act of burning or disrespecting the holy book of the Quran may have direct implications for the lives of foreign workers and ethnic/religious minorities in Afghanistan.

Over the years, I've personally seen how disrespect for the religious beliefs of Afghans and Muslims not only creates animosity all around the world but within international organizations, as well. Some religious Afghans frequently feel offended and disrespected by the news media of high-income countries. You can observe the hard feelings about the disrespect of religious Muslims reflected in their work ethic. This is particularly unfortunate for international development organizations. If you cannot win the hearts of the local people, you'll never win their trust; and hence, you'll never successfully execute your development programs.

One of the most notorious cases of blasphemy involved the murder of a young Afghan woman named Farkhunda. She was a 27-year-old who, according to religious leaders, had burned the Quran. Afghans are quite sensitive to any accusations of blasphemy, true or false, and ended up attacking her. She was stoned, burned, and lynched by a mob in broad daylight. The mob was composed exclusively of all men. One video of the incident showed the mob cheering the lynching. Most of them looked like drug addicts and were observed enjoying the lynching.

Many young Afghan men on the streets of Kabul can appear quite aggressive. Years of conflict have made them lose their compassion and empathy for others. Add poverty to that equation, and people become vulnerable to all kinds of unfortunate influences. Extreme hunger leads people to drugs so they can forget the pains of their daily struggles. In my view, much of the religious extremism and violent thinking also result from drug abuse. Additionally, with drugs so available, this leads to familial and social unrest.

Nevertheless, a mob can display truly frightening levels of aggression and a barbaric mentality when religious issues are involved. In the case of Farkhunda, trials of those persons involved in her murder originally handed down several death sentences, but these were later commuted to a few years in prison. This once again proves that people in high positions can influence Afghan law and that any nefarious act in the name of religion can and often will go unpunished. Criminal accusations against religious leaders (mullahs) are very difficult to prosecute. Mullahs are incredibly influential in the community, often receiving strong support from radical groups of young people.

The lives of people in low-income countries won't improve until they realize they themselves must change. In West Africa, many people are becoming more aware of this. They recognize that many of their old cultural practices can marginalize others and create discrimination, and they understand that not all religious practices are sustainable or ethical. Certain aspects of their current ways of life go against the greater good and must be discarded. On the other hand, those given to extreme religious thinking will continue to judge and treat others as inherently less equal.

Policies And Initiatives

In Afghanistan, all developmental policies must be implemented within a religious context— passages from the Quran justify every policy. This requirement hampers the implementation of many policies that have proven successful in other countries. Because of the lack of perceived flexibility in the interpretation of laws, they are impracticable in Afghanistan. It is an Islamic country, and most if not all of its GDP comes from international development grants. These grants have their intellectual foundations in the ideas of influential Europeans and North Americans who may not know much about the country's religious context.

Many individuals and organizations from high-income countries have attempted various initiatives for the development of Afghanistan, but the country's population generally seems unwilling to accept them. Over the past 200 years, the country has been invaded by the Sikhs from Punjab in India (1837–1838), the British (1838–1842, 1878–1880, and 1919), the Russians (1929, 1930, and 1979), and the United States and NATO (2001). Being a target for so long has made the Afghan people extremely pistanthrophobic—fearful of trusting people due to past experiences and relationships gone wrong.

And who can blame them when foreign powers have so often used Afghanistan for personal gain?

You can see some of the same fear in the population of Western Africa, but native discontent against the influence of high-income countries is much greater in Afghanistan. It appears as though the Afghan people have completely lost trust in all foreign powers, even if their mission is to alleviate the country's poverty and assist Afghans in their struggle to achieve higher standards of living.

Sharing Religious Beliefs

I recall visiting a local church in Côte d'Ivoire. Some people were very fascinated to see me, a foreigner. Some showed concern for my wellbeing and invited me to sit in the front row of the congregation. The celebrant of the service announced my presence, and everyone welcomed me. Unlike in a typical church in Europe or North America, churches in West Africa usually include dancing and singing in their services.

Prayer is a celebration and, for many of the congregants, is an anticipated form of entertainment to which they look forward. However, there were a few people outside the church who did not appear happy to have a foreigner in their midst. One of these individuals even vocalized his annoyance to the others for allowing a white person (in Côte d'Ivoire, brown people are perceived as white) in their church.

This feeling of animosity towards outsiders, I believe, originated when colonial-era Europeans expressed disdain and worse toward Africans who sought entry into European churches. Some of that behavior even persists today. For years, Africans have suffered direct or indirect discrimination in Europe and North America.

This has led many Africans to pay all foreigners in the same coin. Fortunately, however, changing beliefs and a greater appreciation for ethnic and religious diversity have blunted this divisive trend. One example of this came about through the election of Barack Obama as President of the United States. Many Africans rejoiced in this, as they saw him as one of them.

For many in Afghanistan and quite a few in African countries, as well, converting another person to one's religion is a point of pride. Preaching is a way of life for many who believe that if during their lifetime, they can convert at least one person to their religion, they are doing the work of God.

Therefore, many ordinary people do what they can to influence foreigners to join their religion. You'll see signs of this mindset. This occurs through random conversations with strangers on public transport or other places. Strangers will be asked about what religion they follow. If theirs is a religion other than that of the person they are speaking with, that person will promote their religion, explaining how their beliefs are the only way to heaven.

In my experience, arguing about religion in such a context is never a good idea, especially in Afghanistan. If you don't agree with the religious beliefs of others, there is no benefit in speaking against them. It is better to simply not touch the subject unless you share the same religious values. Such talk may lead to accusations of blasphemy and get you into major trouble. This goes even for conversations with your closest colleagues, even if they don't appear to be religious at all. Simply, when traveling, you'll want to adopt this rule: *Do not argue about religion with anyone.*

If you happen to be in a public place in Afghanistan, never display any token of your religion—especially if you are Christian, Hindu, etc. If you're in a conversation with someone, and you sense that person has extreme views about his religion, the best thing you can do is to steer the conversation in another direction. Keep in mind that religion is so important for the people of Afghanistan that they can become upset if, during prayer times, others are engaged in activities other than prayer. If someone misses a prayer, their colleagues may judge them. If you are out and about in an Afghan village during prayer times, you may be stopped by angry people who might even physically abuse you for not praying.

The Afghan culture ingrains religion into its people from childhood. They identify with it as much as they do with the land itself. And so, after suffering repeated invasions as they have, following their religion is a point of national pride and culture.

Appearance

In Afghanistan, a man's facial hair carries immense importance. Long facial hair indicates that a man has a wealth of experience and/or is a religious figure. Practically all-male elders in rural Afghanistan wear a long beard with no mustache. This is a typical look for most religious leaders, as well. Many men start keeping a beard after their pilgrimage visit to Makkah and Medina, the holiest places in Islam.

During Taliban rule, when the organization issued strict guidelines by which everyone had to abide, men were required to keep a beard, as the Taliban prohibited shaving. So, beards were the norm for a while. After Taliban reign ceased, however, barbershops became one of the most common businesses on the streets of Kabul. This became a sign of freedom, and men were suddenly more expressive about their physical appearances.

During my time in Afghanistan, younger men were mostly clean-shaven, while the older men typically kept their beards. The reason most young men are now reluctant to grow a beard may seem strange to persons unfamiliar with Afghan culture, so I will explain. As I said, growing a beard is a sign of religious enlightenment or strong devotion, while shaving one's beard indicates disrespect for or repudiation of Islam. Many young men realize that if they decide to grow their beards for any reason, changing their minds later and shaving them off could bring seriously negative consequences on their lives, so they simply decide not to grow facial hair in the first place.

Similarly, practically every Afghan woman from her school days onward must wear a hijab. Schools insist on this as part of their dress codes. Now, Islamic scholars may debate whether the hijab is obligatory for Muslim women, but in Afghanistan, if a local woman decides not to wear her hijab, that decision could have deadly consequences for her and/or her family. Religious leaders take her rejection of the hijab as a sign that the woman has left the Islam faith and will condemn her for it. I have since learned that many Afghan women, after they immigrate to Western Europe or North America, may no longer wear a hijab and are relieved and pleased to be able to express themselves more freely through their dress.

In some areas of Afghanistan, a burqa (similar in some respects to the hijab but different in that it covers a woman's entire face with mesh netting, including her eyes) is typical attire for women in public. Wearing the burqa was mandatory during Taliban rule, yet even now, several years after the departure of Taliban power, the blue burqa still dominates women's clothing in Afghanistan.

I've heard that wearing a burqa is quite an uncomfortable experience, as it covers a woman from head to toe. Sadly, women must get used to it. Among other discomforts, the burqa blocks the woman's peripheral vision, and you can imagine how extremely uncomfortable it must be during the scorching hot summer months. Women who choose not to wear a burqa out in public are frequently the target of vicious stares and verbal abuse by men. Afghan society has strong cultural norms. Anyone who does not fit in or chooses to display unconventional attitudes may be subjected to severe shaming and discouragement.

In Ghana and Côte d'Ivoire, the hijab is not as common as it is in Afghanistan. West African women have more liberty in terms of choosing their attire. The hijab is most common among conservative communities in Ghana, but overall, I observed that in general, one could not distinguish Christians from Muslims by their dress in rural sub-Saharan Africa. Traditional African block-print material is quite common for clothing. People typically have that material tailored to their preferences. African clothing is extremely colorful and bright, whereas in Afghanistan, one seldom sees brightly-colored clothing, and one rarely sees an Afghan woman in public wearing bright colors.

Alcohol Consumption

Islam prohibits the consumption of alcohol. This prohibition extends into the laws of all Islamic countries. When the Taliban ruled Afghanistan, they imposed the death penalty not only for alcohol consumption but for its mere possession. As of this writing, 16 countries, including Afghanistan, have bans against any kind of alcoholic beverage. Violating these laws leaves one subject to the severe punishments prescribed in Sharia law. Those caught drinking may be fined, imprisoned, or lashed 60 times with a whip.

Despite the many laws banning alcohol in Afghanistan, it is still available at underground parties in Kabul and other big cities. One can usually obtain alcohol at military bases and diplomatic compounds, as well, as restrictions governing those areas are different. Most expatriates in Kabul who enjoy drinking manage to keep alcohol in their homes. One can usually find one's favorite brands. In addition, smugglers bring quite a bit of vodka in from Tajikistan, Russia, and other central Asian countries into Afghanistan. These regional sources are usually more available and less expensive than the brands familiar to Europeans and North Americans.

Church

Similar to Afghanistan, religion plays a big role in most African countries, as well. I noticed that most taxis in Côte d'Ivoire bear the message *Dieu est Bon* (God is Good) on their bumpers. During my time in African countries, I visited many churches, sometimes out of devotion but often out of respect for my hosts. African Christians frequently visit their churches, almost as if this were a recreational activity. Their ceremonies involve people wearing beautiful traditional outfits, dancing, and singing traditional songs. Many follow their religion blindly without thinking critically about the preaching they hear. Consequently, criticizing another's religion can sometimes have deadly consequences.

During my visits to these churches, I invariably saw the priest request donations for the church in the name of God. Many times, these entreaties took the form of a narrative in which a local person had donated all his money to the church and then became extremely successful. Evidently, the emotional appeal of this narrative is quite strong, as I heard it in practically every church I visited.

I recall a specific incident during a religious ceremony in Tamale, Ghana. Here, the priests called donors to come forward, summoning them in the order of their donation's value from the highest to the lowest. After the priests called out someone's name and the amount this person was about to donate, the person would come forward with that amount in their hands and put the money in a big box. The whole congregation would then break out in a round of applause.

Then the priests would call out another name and smaller donation, and that person would do as the previous donor had done until the performance ended with donations of two *cedis* (about one U.S. dollar). With each donation, the enthusiasm of the congregation's applause reflected the progressively smaller amounts.

During this ceremony, the priests would encourage the congregation even to donate their lunch money to God, sometimes repeating fearful stories (which occasionally originated in movies) of people who did not worship God and therefore ended up poor and miserable.

Membership in a church benefits many people, as it provides a sense of community and acceptance from others. But it can also reinforce socioeconomic stratification when people who cannot afford large donations to their church receive less respect in the community than those who flaunt their large donations.

There was another time when a priest in Abidjan, Côte d'Ivoire, invited me to his house. I had attended mass at his church on the previous day, and I listened to all the stories in his homily, taking them as lessons regarding how to live a good life for the benefit of others. At times, he spoke negatively about atheists and people who followed other religions, saying that they would all end up burning in hell.

But he always came back to the point that praising God and showing Him how devoted you are the most important things in life—how one should never luxuriate in material comforts but rather devote the best of one's energy toward serving the church. At the time, it didn't appear to me that this was a problem at that church, as so many of the congregants were extremely poor people, to begin with.

I was honored and pleased when the priest invited me to his house, but I have to admit I was surprised and shocked when I arrived and witnessed his lifestyle. He lived in quite a nice house, had five children, a car, and all the material comforts that pass for luxury in African cities. It didn't look as if he or his family faced the same sort of shortages and struggles that members of his congregation were facing. Frankly, seeing some religious leaders preaching the extreme sacrifice of the little money one might have in the name of God when most of these religious leaders themselves lived very comfortable lives appeared a bit hypocritical to me.

I noticed a similar dynamic in Afghanistan. Many religious leaders appear to use religion hypocritically, encouraging members of their congregations to sacrifice much of the little they have to support the comfortable lifestyles of the leaders and their families. Of course, there also are others who live as they preach, but the ones who do not end up degrading the credibility and reputations of those who do.

Many Afghans want a change from the current corrupt religious regime. Some of these individuals, and some from Pakistan as well, have taken to advocating for secularism and even atheism. They typically do this in secret, using fake Facebook or other social media accounts to spread their ideas. Many of these forward-thinking Afghans concentrate on the country's educational system, criticizing its policy of not challenging any religious teachings. Many if not all of these people are eager to leave the country, but finding no real opportunities to do so, they seek ways to improve the status quo from within.

Ramadan

Ramadan, the ninth month of the Islamic calendar, is the holiest month of the year for Muslims around the world. It is the month of fasting. Everywhere I've lived, I have met Muslims who observe the strict fast this month requires. This fast includes abstaining from all food and drink, the use of tobacco, sexual relations, and any sinful behavior. It lasts from sunrise to sunset throughout the month and is obligatory for all adult Muslims except those who are acutely or chronically ill, traveling, menstruating, pregnant, breastfeeding, or elderly.

The Islamic calendar is lunar, so its months progress at a different pace than those of the common solar calendar and therefore may fall within any season. The fast can be extremely difficult during the summer with its hot weather and longer days, especially for those engaged in outdoor physical labor. During Ramadan, Muslims are encouraged to transform the discomfort of the fast into devotion, prayer, and the recitation of the Quran.

I have been fortunate and fascinated to have witnessed Ramadan both in Islamic and non-Islamic countries. In Côte d'Ivoire and Ghana, which are Christian-majority countries, everyday activities proceed as usual during Ramadan. You'll still see vibrancy on the streets. People are still hustling and bustling around the clock to make their livelihoods. Only the Muslim population is fasting. In the evening, you may see more people around restaurants or mosques, but overall, your life doesn't change very much if you are not Muslim. Individuals who have Muslim coworkers may show them more consideration because of the fast, but productivity is essentially the same as it would be during any other part of the year.

In Afghanistan, however, my experience of Ramadan was vastly different than it was anywhere else. Working hours at the office changed considerably. My Afghan coworkers arrived as early as seven or eight o'clock in the morning and left for the day by noon or one o'clock. When Ramadan occurred during the summer heat, I suspected that many secretly dreaded its approach, as the fast makes working in the heat extremely difficult.

During the hottest hours of the day, almost everyone who is able goes home and naps or otherwise rests until sunset. When the announcement comes from the mosque that the sun has officially set, people break their fasts by slowly drinking water and sometimes eating a few dates. At length, they finally have a meal. After that, people are more active and do more things around the house. I even observed more emails going out in the evenings than throughout the day.

Observant Muslims then take their night's rest, rising at about three or four a.m. so they can have a meal just before sunrise when they'll commence fasting again. During the day, the streets are mostly empty, with only a few stores open. Of course, that description changes somewhat depending on the season in which Ramadan falls.

There is less hardship when the weather is cooler, and the days are shorter.

Ramadan is the month Afghans devote entirely to religion while other aspects of their lives take a step back. Practically no one schedules work deadlines during that month, and if they do, no one really expects them to be met. Perhaps because of this slower work pace, most non-Muslim foreign workers leave Afghanistan during Ramadan. Another reason for this exodus is that often fasting Afghans have less patience than they do during the rest of the year. Many tend to be easily angered while fasting. People tend to be more overtly religious during Ramadan. Enforcement of prayer becomes stricter.

I remember once going through security and immigration at the Kabul airport during Ramadan, and uniformed personnel openly referred to me as a *kaffir* (infidel). I suspect some of them were Afghans who had lived in Pakistan and developed an antipathy toward Indians. Airport security and immigration duties can be difficult jobs during Ramadan, so people with those responsibilities tend to be irritable and short-tempered at that time.

My Afghan colleagues were quite considerate toward me and other foreigners who did not observe the fast. Even during Ramadan, they offered me proper meals in my residential compound. However, in respect to their religion, I would always eat privately in my room or in my office behind a locked door. I would never drink or eat in front of them.

In general, I found the efforts of most fasting Muslims commendable, but I also observed some who appeared rankled by their society's pressure on them to fast. I also heard of some cases in which the families of pregnant women forced them to fast, and in Taliban-controlled areas, people who were caught inappropriately breaking their fast suffered severe punishments and even incarceration. However, this was rare because Afghans who do not observe the fast do their eating and drinking as secretly as possible.

As per some of my colleagues, I learned the typical punishment for breaking the Ramadan fast in some Afghan villages involves being put on a donkey with a message in front saying, "I broke the fast." Such naming and shaming are quite common in many places in Afghanistan.

If a foreign Muslim is working in Afghanistan and that person's religious upbringing was perhaps not as strict as the typical Afghan's, they could be in for a hard time. They may have been brought up with a looser understanding of the Ramadan fast, but Afghans see them only as bad Muslims if they don't follow Afghanistan's fasting traditions. Being treated that way, some of these foreign workers end up feeling quite guilty for not being good Muslims. Many Afghans consciously or unconsciously encourage expatriate Muslims to obey Afghanistan's Islamic traditions while in the country. I took this as unintentional behavior, but with the entire society following a strict set of traditions, it can be very difficult to go against the norms.

All that being said, non-Muslims residing in Afghanistan should do their best to keep their personal religious views and practices to themselves, especially during Ramadan, when the general religious fervor is at its most acute. Keep a low profile concerning your religion and be discreet about it. In public places and on TV, one frequently hears that Islam is the only religion that grants one access to heaven. Don't argue against that view even if you believe otherwise. Religion is an extremely sensitive topic in this country—people are willing to die and kill for it.

In contrast, Muslims in other countries of Central Asia have a much more relaxed attitude toward Ramadan. In Uzbekistan and Tajikistan, all offices are open as usual. People still go about their daily activities, and alcohol is still available. One could easily forget that it's Ramadan, even though both countries have majority Muslim populations. Many Afghans who live in Tajikistan or Uzbekistan don't fast during Ramadan, as the obligation to strictly follow all of Islam's rules is not as strong in those neighboring countries. When Afghans are abroad, and away from the constant surveillance of religious neighbors and police, they have more liberty to choose how closely they will follow this way of life.

Secularism In Neighboring Countries

In Afghanistan, it is unsafe to preach or practice other faiths openly. Similar phenomena are also witnessed in communities such as Uzbekistan and Tajikistan. Although people appear more tolerant in both of these countries, preaching against any religion is negatively perceived by their governments. Those who preach their faith mostly do so in tight circles or on the internet under anonymous names.

The governments of Tajikistan and Uzbekistan understand the repercussions of strict Islamic laws and life, particularly after observing the recent history of Iran, Afghanistan, and Pakistan. These countries have majority Muslim populations, but their strongest cultural influence is not from Islam but from Russia and the former Soviet Union, which is secular. These governments have strict laws and policies concerning political and cultural extremism, and understandably so. During the Soviet era, the KGB kept the religious proclivities of these countries in tight check, and its successor (the Federal Security Service, or FSB) continues to closely monitor the ebbs and flows of religious fervor there.

Tajikistan and Uzbekistan's intelligence and security agencies monitor all foreigners who enter from Afghanistan, Pakistan, Iran, and other strict Islamic countries during their stay for signs of attempts to spread extremism. They take note of actions, including often going to the mosque, wearing the entire Islamic veil, or speaking about the virtues of Sharia law. Such activities may lead to trouble with the authorities.

If someone goes about in Tajikistan wearing the traditional Afghan salwar kameez or a full burqa, the police will regularly contact and question that person. The two countries have either discouraged or altogether banned hijabs in schools, so children come to understand the importance of secularism and develop a moderate approach toward religious views. This is vital because if either of these countries were to become conservative and religiously strict, the path to secularism and a more liberal lifestyle would likely vanish. I say this mindful of the recent history of Iran, Afghanistan, and Pakistan—many people in those countries suffer from extreme religious ideologies, especially women and religious minorities.

Religious Harmony

Developing and maintaining harmony among religious groups is crucial for world peace, but especially so in countries with religiously diverse populations. During my days in Ghana, the proportion of Christians in the overall population was about 70 percent, with Islam being the second-most prevalent religion. However, most Ghanaian Muslims live in the northern part of the country, so the government does its best to maintain harmony between religions, as the country's development depends on avoiding religious conflict.

Ghana is a religious country. Every meeting, conference, or training—especially in rural areas—starts and ends with a prayer. Ghanaians also realize that all religions deserve respect and that this is the way to maintain social harmony amongst all religious communities. For example, if the opening prayer at a meeting is Islamic, the closing prayer will be Christian. This way, everyone knows that society acknowledges and respects the presence of her or his religion. It also signals that society values peace and pluralism.

In Ghana and Côte d'Ivoire, people spend as much as they can afford on clothes for Sunday church services—far more than they would ever spend on school or work clothes. I frequently saw people reading the Bible in public transport, and many even loudly recited Bible verses in public. People take this sort of behavior as a sign of dedication to Jesus, positively viewing any person with a Bible. In Western Africa, anyone who shows extraordinary dedication to their religion always receives a kind appreciation for their religious behavior.

In Afghanistan, of course, the situation is different, as it is in other countries of Central Asia. During my time in that part of the world, meetings would open and close only after a reading of verses from the Quran. This is because Islam is the official state religion of Afghanistan and the country's population is 99.7 percent Muslim.

At these times, any non-Muslim participant need not join in the prayer, but custom demands that any participant who does not pray must show respect for Islam by keeping silent during the reading from the Quran. All women, irrespective of their religion, must keep their heads covered during the reading from the Quran at the start of every event. Foreign women unfamiliar with Afghan culture sometimes encounter trouble because of this custom. No Afghan person would ever tell a foreign woman to cover her head, but all understand that women who leave their heads uncovered during a reading from the Quran are displaying disrespect to Islam.

Man or woman who follows the second pillar of Islam (to pray five times a day) and complies with Islamic etiquette to the letter receives great respect from everyone. Although some habitually disregard the spirit of Islam in their private lives, if they appear in the community to be following Islam's call, they will receive respect in that community. In fact, you can see the same phenomenon practically everywhere. Many regular churchgoers, and even many prominent leaders of congregations, behave in their private lives in ways their religions prohibit.

Christian missionaries have been a big target of violence in Afghanistan. Even though in recent years, the Afghan government has passed laws to protect religious minorities, officials rarely enforce them. Almost all Afghans consider their country's religion to be the supreme authority. By contrast, residents of Ghana and Côte d'Ivoire enjoy much greater freedom of religion. You can observe churches and mosques of various sects and religions other than Christianity and Islam, also enjoying their places of meeting and worship out in the open.

Afghan politicians win their votes by promising that all of Afghanistan will be a land of Islamic law. The more religious a political party's appeal, the more support they receive. Most Islamic countries provide very little freedom for religious minorities to practice their religions. Some have expelled non-Muslims or condoned forced conversions, leaving the remaining religious minorities living in constant fear of their security and wellbeing. In Afghanistan, such practices have damaged the country's reputation as people think of it as a country unable to protect its minorities.

In Afghanistan, one can also see the growing influence of Wahhabism, a particularly strict Islamic doctrine and religious movement that originated more than two hundred years ago in Saudi Arabia. From a western perspective, Wahhabism's practice involves massive violations of human rights, but its evangelists are very well-financed.

Unfortunately, its influence is growing in several Central Asian countries where people are becoming more radicalized and religious. Some national governments have resisted its growth, but individuals and groups in Saudi Arabia extravagantly and relentlessly fund its spread. To combat its growth, those governments will have to closely monitor their societies for increasing radicalism.

In conversations with extremely religious Afghans, I found that anything they could construe as contradicting Islam could lead to aggressive and even violent behavior, so remember never to argue about religion in Afghanistan. One reason for this might be that in Islamic countries such as Afghanistan and Pakistan, children don't learn much about other religions in school. Hence, you'll find an extremely low tolerance for other religions.

Apostasy in Islam is commonly defined as the conscious abandonment of Islam by a Muslim in word or through a deed. As of 2014, apostasy was a capital offense in Afghanistan. It is far from unknown to have communities and even families lynching one of their own people for contradicting common religious beliefs.

Many people believe that a college education tends to open one's mind to various points of view about many topics, but even educated people can hold a strict conservative and narrow-minded approach concerning people of different religions, races, etc. This is a world-wide phenomenon. My view is that traveling to diverse countries and meeting people from different cultures is what really opens one's mind. It is a special kind of education that teaches you to accept people who look and behave differently than you.

Chapter 7.

Business Culture and Work Ethics

For a variety of reasons, it's commonly believed that people in low-income and conflict-torn countries don't work as hard as those that live in more stable parts of the world. This belief supposedly explains the low quality of life in those countries that experience political instability. However, based on my personal experience, this belief is a myth.

During my time abroad, I witnessed many of my colleagues working much harder than many people I met in high-income countries. In Afghanistan, many of my colleagues would work after office hours, especially those involved with security and intelligence. Most of them were always on alert in case of an attack.

In most middle and low-income countries, unemployment and underemployment are very common. The frequent possibility of armed conflict also destroys employment opportunities and local infrastructure. In addition, with no minimum wage standard set by the government, many people work long hours for barely enough remuneration to meet even the most basic needs of their families.

Many members of the workforce, even those with university degrees, must resort to measures such as selling vegetables in the market or perform basic physical labor during the weekends. The struggle to maintain an adequate quality of life is often overwhelming. Governments provide no safety nets like social security or minimum wage standards. Many people work in family businesses, as the risk and struggle associated with doing something outside the family structure is much greater than it would be in high-income countries. Young adults who decide not to take over the family business are often considered disrespectful and rebellious.

Consequently, many people can't achieve their higher ambitions by pursuing a career that they're passionate about. Many very talented people don't become artists or professional athletes due to the risk that they won't be able to support themselves later in life.

Other factors also influence the development of a thriving business culture in low-income countries. In Afghanistan, I saw many products for sale in local stores that were way past their 'best used by' date. This is partly because the product labels are in English, and few local people understand the language. Naturally, this leads to adverse health issues for the people who consume these foods.

I also noticed that there was an abundance of products manufactured in China on display in Afghan and West African supermarkets. China appears to have flooded the markets of low-income and conflict-torn countries with their food products. They're able to do this because of the products' low prices, which is also an indicator of quality.

Chinese companies also imitate the labels of well-known and high-quality brands. These forgeries are usually so accurate that one must inspect them very closely in order to recognize them as such. China even exports obsolete vehicles to Afghanistan. Vehicles that would never be allowed on the roads in China are a common sight on the roads of Afghanistan. Many Chinese-manufactured trucks break down on the mountainous and narrow Afghan roads, resulting in miles-long traffic jams that can often last for hours in hazardous weather. In West Africa, Chinese workers are a ubiquitous sight because Chinese companies win so many construction contracts in that part of the world.

When it comes to starting a business, the experience can be intimidating no matter where you are in the world. I've met many very ambitious people, all eager to commence their startups with high hopes and dreams. Practically every country has provisions and tax breaks in place that are designed to encourage people to move forward with their initiatives. Many new businesses fail within a year or two, but many also become successful. The culture of entrepreneurship in high-income countries can differ vastly from a similar culture in other economies. In conflict-torn areas, the price of starting a business can be extremely high because of the associated security issues.

In low-income countries, very many people live in poverty and struggle on a daily basis. As a result, any flaunting of wealth can be dangerous to those people doing so, as well as to their families. For example, in Afghanistan, kidnapping and extortion are relatively commonplace. Consequently, international companies are extremely cautious about opening operations there. It, therefore, follows that employment opportunities are harder to come by than they otherwise would be. In turn, the lack of honest employment opportunities results in an atmosphere of crime and mayhem that further deters international companies from operating in the country. In other words, it's a vicious cycle that involves few employment opportunities, conditions that encourage crime, and reluctance on the part of international companies to invest in Afghanistan.

However, Afghanistan can boast of some success stories involving new businesses and successful businessmen. Executives for such businesses generally run their operations from Dubai or other cities outside Afghanistan. This reduces the considerable risk of the executives or their family members being kidnapped.

Businesses operating in Afghanistan spend an incredible amount on security to keep their personnel and other assets safe. The largest businesses have their headquarters in Kabul or situated in a few other big cities, conducting their manual operations and obtaining their raw materials from rural areas.

Afghanistan's native industries include textiles, soap, furniture, shoes, fertilizer, apparel, natural gas, coal, copper, mineral water, and cement. However, the most common and profitable business in Afghanistan involves the export of fresh and dried fruit. Afghanistan has an abundance of very high-quality fruits, including pomegranates and apples, along with dried fruits such as raisins, apricots, figs, cherries, prunes, dates, and mulberries.

Dried fruit from Afghanistan is very easy to find in parts of the Middle East and India. Afghanistan also produces very high-quality saffron that sells for very high prices in other countries. For example, in Europe and North America, saffron sells for more than ten times the price it can command in rural Afghanistan. A portion of the mark-up involves paying bribes to corrupt government officials in order to secure the required export authorizations. Unfortunately, the profits made with Afghan fresh and dried fruit make the business attractive for fraudsters. Much of the saffron and many of the other spices you might find in your local market that's supposed to be 'imported from Afghanistan' may not be authentic.

Other businesses, such as furniture, textiles, and especially carpets, are also profitable. Afghan carpets are unique and are often beautiful works of art. They are mostly handmade, and the finer the material, such as silk, the higher the price. Afghan refugees living in Pakistan weave many of these carpets. Prices range from less than fifty to thousands of dollars, depending on the carpet's size and quality.

Many carry the image of Afghan politician and military commander Ahmad Shah Massoud, and these are intended as wall hangings. Carpets can also be made to order. These take time to weave, but of course, each one is unique. The Afghan regions of Mazar-e-sharif and Herat produce carpets that command high prices around the world.

Tax avoidance is very prevalent among businesses that are established in low as well as in high-income countries. In low-income areas, taxes are generally quite low, but the system still tends to take from the poor and subsidize the better off in society. This sort of tax structure is largely responsible for the prevalence of intractable income inequality.

All bigger businesses naturally seek friends in government, finding them through a variety of means, from networking to bribery. Emboldened by their allies in government and a general lack of transparency, many businesses declare losses rather than the profits they earn. In addition, with the low cost of manual labor and with workers so abundant, the employees sometimes earn barely enough to keep body and soul together.

High unemployment means that most of those that are employed have no job security. Workers can be fired without notice or severance pay. This leads to members of society paying great respect, often unearned, to managers working for larger companies who have the ability to hire and fire workers at will.

Few laws protect employees who have been fired from their jobs, while even the few workers' rights that do exist are rarely enforced by the state. If a worker decides to sue the employer concerning their salary or working conditions, the courts might take years to hear the case. Meanwhile, lawyers' fees and other administrative charges accumulate, so most efforts to address these grievances come to nothing.

Another factor to consider is the ownership structure in low-income countries. In these parts of the world, the ownership of many businesses is often hereditary, passing from father to son. In many cases, this works out well for the son, but some young men chafe at the pressure to take over their father's businesses, especially if they think they can do better for themselves in another occupation.

Unfortunately, daughters almost never inherit their father's businesses. This is because in these countries, women are usually not considered to be strong enough to handle the business environment. Yet, in recent years, many very capable African and Asian businesswomen have bucked the old trend, although these businesses led by women tend to be new ventures. If the male proprietor of a family business only has female children, he'll often pass on the business to one of his daughter's husbands. As you'd expect, this practice leads some unethical men to court the daughters of business owners who have no sons. That way, the men can assume the inheritance of another family.

In Afghanistan, small and medium-sized enterprises are the lifeblood of the Afghan economy and have proved instrumental in creating income-generating opportunities for people. These businesses employ from 10 to 500 people. Many are based in big cities such as Kabul, Mazar-e-Sharif, Herat, Kandahar, Ghazni, Jalalabad, Kunduz, Fayzabad, Maimana, Jowzjan, and Taloqan. Many are owned by women and manufacture handicrafts or carpets. Similarly, in Ghana, I saw a number of such businesses providing employment for widows and other marginalized people.

The business worlds of Asia and Africa are still raw. They have a high potential for expansion, with their governments often offering tax benefits to foreign corporations. This creates enormous potential for foreigners seeking to generate income in the country. There are constant risks of fraud, but these risks can be dealt with by working with a few reliable locals who are smart enough to identify and handle such issues. The locals can also more effectively deal with the local bureaucracies.

Compared to the rest of Africa, and especially other countries in Western Africa, Ghana has been doing much better because of its economic and political stability. As a result, many foreign corporations have established operations there. In the capital, Accra, one can see many international restaurants, malls, and showrooms. Accra has grown and prospered at a much faster rate than Abidjan, the capital of Côte d'Ivoire, mainly due to the security of the country. Côte d'Ivoire has suffered from several civil conflicts in recent years.

Another factor that comes into play in entrepreneurship is interethnic discrimination. Employers will often hire people that belong to the same ethnic or religious groups like themselves, rather than basing their decision solely on a person's education, experience, or suitability for the position.

Many well-established business people have either been discriminated against at their workplace or have run into the glass ceiling of nepotism. Employers frequently offer jobs to family members rather than to those candidates that are the most qualified for the role, making it very difficult for people to find suitable employment.

When people feel discriminated against or find employment, the most ambitious take this as an opportunity to start a business of their own. Many people start their tailoring or barbershops, or open general stores, and so on. Afghanistan has very few supermarkets and big-box stores, so much of the business that occurs in these types of locations in high-income countries takes place in smaller shops in Afghanistan. Residents know where to go to find what they need. Naturally, this involves a certain amount of inconvenience, buying different things from a number of different shops, but small businesses also provide many jobs within the local economy.

Furthermore, successful businesses in low-income countries require a lot of networking with bourgeois culture. Although people in high-income countries often say that 'clothes don't make the man', the polar opposite applies in low-income countries when it comes to businesses. Businesspeople and entrepreneurs must either flaunt their wealth or fake it to win the trust of investors and other businesspeople. No matter where you are in the world, business culture is about winning the trust of others, and past achievements in the business environment only go so far in that regard. One's standard of living, including how many cars and houses one owns or the price of one's watch, can be much more convincing, especially when one is networking for the purpose of selling business proposals.

Overall, entrepreneurs in low-income countries must work much harder to gain the confidence of people in order to stand out from the scammers and reduce or eliminate reliance on the judicial systems for the redress of fraud and other crimes.

In Afghanistan, despite the disasters occurring in different areas of the country, it's not all dangerous. Some cities are relatively safe and bear little resemblance to the war-torn communities that are so frequently publicized in the media. Some of these communities are safe to the point that anyone can consider them for establishing a business and engaging in tourism. Raw materials are profitably traded, and rich cultural heritage is upheld in these communities.

Fig. 13 Chinese products flooded in Afghan markets. These are deodorants in Kabul named iPhone and Facebook.

Fig. 14 Chinese products in Ghana. This is a phone charger named G8 Summit.

Chapter 8.

Corruption Scenarios

Corruption, or abuse of privilege by influential individuals, is a phenomenon with a centuries-long history, debasing every country to this day. When corruption occurs at the top levels of national power, it can destroy a nation's progress.

Its prevalence is a notably significant difference between high-and low-income countries, as almost every country has the necessary resources to obtain general prosperity. All too often, when armed conflict erupts in a country, law and order degrade, and the officials who vowed to enforce the country's laws become offenders themselves. When this transpires, and authorities exploit the rights of others, law and order collapse.

During my field visits, it became clear that corruption is a critical element that hollows out a country's economy and destroys the trust of the persons in their leadership. I witnessed several incidents in Afghanistan, Uzbekistan, Tajikistan, Ghana, Côte d'Ivoire, etc., in which cash payments were required for services that the citizens shouldn't have to pay for. Even countries that might be otherwise poor in natural resources have the means to boost their economies to the benefit of their citizens; they can develop their tourism industry, for example.

Corruption is a norm in many countries and conflict-torn regions. Police, military, government officials, and others responsible for implementing and enforcing the law are themselves the biggest culprits. In Uzbekistan and Tajikistan, harassment by the local police on the streets is not an uncommon occurrence. On the other hand, in Ghana and Côte d'Ivoire, police corruption is not as overt as in Uzbekistan and Tajikistan. The police and security tend to be more amicable than in Central Asian countries.

All administrative work, such as getting a driver's license or having a passport issued, can take several days unless they get a kickback for faster service. Sometimes, it's impossible to get your birth certificate or police clearances without bribing the officers.

The amount depends on the officer's rank, but higher-level officials often share the proceeds through the tiers of bureaucracy to the bottom level in reverse-pyramid style. In other words, if the top official is corrupt, there will be no need to deal with lower personnel to accomplish the task. Albeit's high-level corruption also denotes that a country is approaching an economic disaster.

At any point, as you interact with figures of authority, do not bribe anyone. Even if they demand it, maintain your ground and dare to report them. As an international staff member, your complaint will be treated more seriously than ones from the citizens. Pay the fine for the blunders committed rather than bribe an officer. This is the only way not to subsidize the doctrines already threatening their transparency and development.

Corruption is like a pest decimating a country, but if it's confined to lower levels, the country suffers less impairment. When high-level officials are honest and dedicated, they can often take steps against lower-level dishonesty. Eliminating it can be a slow process, but if the leaders set a good example, lower-level officials will oblige sooner or later. However, when the highest levels of government are tainted, having honest, and dedicated employees at the bottom are ineffective. Those who enter government or financial businesses at a low or middle level almost always become a part of the corruption cycle. Their meager salaries motivate them to profit more through kickbacks.

For a country to progress for the benefit of its citizens, a strong work ethic is vital. Yet when a country's government is rampant with nepotism, the essential transformation must come from the top. Individuals in public service or security in developing countries will observe corruption at various levels. Bribery is so common in many government offices in Afghanistan and Ghana; it gives one the impression that it's a lawful practice.

This means that honest people who prefer not to go along with the status quo cannot affect a change for the better because everyone else is part of the system. Corruption runs through government services from top to bottom, with everyone getting their share. Whistleblowers are ineffective because the success of their efforts depends on honesty at higher levels in the bureaucracy, or at least in the media, and seldom can it be found.

Furthermore, whistleblowers comprehend they will face retaliation such as being fired, and a loss of income could be disastrous for them and their families. Still, corrupt government officials dread whistleblowers, and this leads them to fill low-level jobs in their bureaucracies with individuals who have confirmed their obedience and contentment with the existing status quo.

Another facet that enables corruption in underprivileged and war-torn countries is the high degree of authority, and respect employers typically have. The concept of employee rights is quite frail in these areas, so some proprietors abuse their privilege, and in many places, the threat of being dismissed can be intense due to high unemployment rates. I witnessed incidents of sexual harassment and other ill-treatment during my time in the field, even though most international organizations have policies concerning the abuse of personnel, and most employees feel secure enough.

These problems have no relation to ethnicity or nationality. Rather, the lack of proper laws and enforcement of the present laws, combined with the scarcity of opportunities, allow those in power to exploit others. The worst is that war destroys the law and order of a country; it demoralizes the population, who lose hope for a better future. This provides a contingency to take advantage of the situation. It is unlikely that people are born to become a stain on society, but when the circumstance allows it, they inevitably emerge. Otherwise, the human mentality is the same.

While in Tajikistan, I observed the Tajik people, the police, particularly, have a low opinion of Afghan men because some were involved in drug trafficking or sex tourism. On the streets of Dushanbe, the police can be severe with Afghan men, wresting them even when some had legitimate business or professional visits.

The Tajik police can be immoral; in most situations, kickbacks are a norm. Depending on the rank of the officer, it can be as small as three dollars (U.S.). If you are from a diplomatic community or have enough time to prove that you have all the legal documents, however, it's acceptable to answer their "security" questions. The police are often looking for a bribe and harass you with assorted bureaucratic "requirements" that may not even exist.

For instance, even if your passport has a valid visa, they sometimes ask for local registration. And even if you have that, they will request your organization's ID. The more nervous you look, the more they pester. Some would even threaten you with jail, but most of them just look for a bribe. It's always recommended to complain (through your organization) to a higher management level than engage in arguments with street police, who often have limited English-language skills.

Sometimes in Tajikistan, when the police see an Afghan man walking with a Tajik woman, they will harass the couple. In both Uzbekistan and Tajikistan, most resident men disapprove of local women in the company of foreign men, even if the pair are colleagues walking from work together.

As a foreign man in one of these countries, and in the company of a local woman, be prepared to be stopped by the police to question the relationship between you and the woman. This is from personal experience. Once, I was walking in Tajikistan with a local female colleague, the police stopped us and embarrassed my colleague for walking with a foreign man. It's similar in Uzbekistan. I know of one incident was a group of young Uzbek men battered a foreign man who was walking with an unmarried Uzbek woman one early evening. Youth in certain cultures can be hostile and possessive when local women befriend non-citizen males, even if the friendship is platonic.

Of course, Afghan men are aware of this. So when they cross the border into Tajikistan, they do not wear the traditional garb of salwar kameez. Instead, they change into European/North American clothes of pants and dress shirts. They do this not only to avoid being hassled by the police. The Tajik police also routinely harass men that they identify as Afghan for bribes. If you travel from Afghanistan to Tajikistan by road, the bribing culture becomes more prevalent unless you are in an identifiable diplomatic vehicle.

At the border between Afghanistan and Tajikistan, border officials often scrutinize all the luggage and confiscate any weapons. Swiss Army knives seem to be in high demand, so if a Tajik border official finds one in your baggage (that is, not even on your person), he will probably confiscate it. If you have one and want to keep it, either let your Tajik colleague/friend carry it or just don't bring it into the country.

The bribing culture is also common along the borders of West African countries. The requirement to always keep the passport and residency papers with you; however, it is not as enforced as it is in Central Asia. In Central Asian countries, you should always keep your identification documents with you. Locals have their ID cards, and foreigners must always carry their passports or copies of their passports and visas.

I have seen that corruption starts at immigration checkpoints in many countries. Many of the times that I stood in front of an immigration officer who was verifying that the passports and stamps are in order, would ask for a "gift" or a *cadeau* (French for "gift"). This occurs more often if you carry a non-diplomatic passport from a high-income country or if you appear untrained to the country.

Airports create a first impression of the country, and, unfortunately, if immigration officers are impolite, it provides a negative and lasting impression. Most immigration officers in impoverished countries are friendlier than their North American or Western European counterparts, who seem to have an air of superiority when dealing with citizens of underprivileged countries who are about to enter theirs. This arrogance, so common in high-income countries, is unusual in the airport's immigration and customs area of impoverished countries. They may be corrupt and expect bribes, but their overall attitude toward foreigners is more welcoming. The reason might be because many destitute countries have stronger traditions of sociability and hospitality than most well-to-do nations, where people are more reserved.

If an immigration officer asks for money when entering a foreign country, do not feel intimidated and do your best to appear at ease. Most often, they will ask for a little gift; in response, just smile and stay relaxed. From my experience, a friendly demeanor is the best course of action, no matter how the other person treats you at the immigration and customs. Conduct all conversations with courtesy. That is, refuse the request with a smile, and remain calm.

My typical behavior in these circumstances has been to say, "Oh, I am so sorry. I forgot to bring a gift for you, my friend." This approach has always been helpful. Do your best to create a situation where everyone is calm; then, you can enter the country without encouraging the bribe culture. One more issue, as per my experience: Never report corruption issues at the airport as fraud is a norm. Later, report it to your organization or the country's ministry of tourism.

In the baggage-collection area, uniformed officers or airport employees in low-income countries will sometimes offer to carry your luggage. These might be genuine expressions of goodwill, but many times a payment is expected. If you want some help with your luggage, be sure to carry a few one-dollar (U.S.) bills with you if you don't have small denominations in the local currency. Also, negotiate a price prior to the service; otherwise, a larger payment might be expected. Of course, you can also refuse these offers of assistance. But always do so with courtesy.

After you have claimed your bags, several taxi drivers will approach you. Most of them charge a lofty fare. Far more reliable and trustworthy are the airport taxi systems. Yet, you will be better off walking outside the airport and taking a metered taxi, as those don't pay the high taxes. Negotiating reasonable deals with these drivers is also possible.

While employed with the local government in Walewale, Ghana, much of the corruption by senior officials was not reported, or when it was, no charges were filed. This is because all high-ranking officials—from the head doctor to the district assembly governor or the superintendent of education—all know how to deal with the village's police commissioner. As the saying goes: one hand washes the other.

International organizations often have much more transparency than local governments. Albeit when it comes to macro-level projects and program funding, corruption sometimes occurs in the lower levels of the bureaucracy, as when employees fake receipts for reimbursement. Since most slips are handwritten, transparency suffers when a lack of technology limits the ways to verify receipts.

Paid medical bills, for example, are often documented with hand-written notes. Some high-level managers and executives usually try to keep their domestic staff—which includes cook, cleaner, driver, etc.—honest by limiting their periods of employment because so many of them forge grocery bills, automobile fuel, etc. Many also separate the duties of domestic staff to create more transparency. To avoid nepotism, many proprietors also recruit foreigners to ascertain that at least recruitment is based on merit. Foreign workers have few or no ties with ethnic groups or other bases of discrimination.

The unreliability of the judiciary is a foremost reason corruption is rampant in Afghanistan and West African countries. For many reasons, the locals believe it is risky to take up cases against a corrupt political officer. First, they can upturn judgment in their favor, bribe the judge, and go scot-free. Secondly, it is also possible the case gets delayed in court for years before the verdict. In fact, it is not surprising that the locals prefer to settle out of court or let the snag continue to slide.

While crossing borders in West Africa on land, I noticed that the immigration systems are still relatively unorganized. Smugglers move massive amounts of contraband without paying any tariffs, and people as well move relatively freely across international borders without security monitoring. I was once on a bus that crossed the Côte d'Ivoire-Ghana border. After our bus stopped, two customs officers entered. They seemed to be in a hurry, quickly glancing at the people on the bus.

One of the officers pointed at my colleague and me—we were the only non-black travelers on the bus. He asked us to come out and then asked about our plans and our origin. He even jokingly offered wives to us, in case we were interested in hooking up with girls in his country. We were both surprised but just laughed it off. He then asked us for our yellow fever vaccination cards, a requirement for entry into most African countries, and I showed him my valid card.

Unfortunately, my colleague had forgotten his vaccination card. At that point, the officer sent us to another table, and when we got there, another officer looked at my colleague and asked him why he didn't have his card. My colleague said that he had forgotten it back in his room in Abidjan. The unbothered officer then looked at my colleague and asked him for $20, in exchange for which my colleague would receive a new vaccination card.

Since the bus was waiting for us, he didn't argue and paid him $20 and received a new card. The officer went on to say that he had vaccination cards for other diseases as well and wanted to know if we wanted any. My colleague received the card, and when he asked about the actual vaccination, the officer said he didn't have any. Meaning they were literally just handing out vaccination certificates without providing the doses.

We took this all as a joke at that moment, but this is how corruption affects a country. Apparently, many travelers acquire their vaccination cards through this process, which includes no vaccinations. Whether it was yellow fever or polio, customs/immigration officials sell the certificates without providing the service; the certificates were meant to document. These travelers could be disease carriers and go on to infect others with polio or other communicable diseases.

We were only identified because we were the only non-blacks on the bus, meaning it is much easier for criminals of African descent to be able to cross the border into a different country.

Some of the most overwhelming experiences were my visits to orphanages in Ghana, Côte d'Ivoire, and Afghanistan. War and poverty have left masses of orphaned children in Côte d'Ivoire and Afghanistan. These wars also have dispersed members of innumerable families, and with economic collapse, even the children's relatives cannot take care of them. Thus abandoned, they wind up at orphanages. Too many of these institutions are funded by trivial government subsidies or private sector donations, and the kids sometimes suffer physical and sexual abuse.

Unhygienic conditions create further health issues, and many children develop infirmities due to deficient care. Many have had scant, if any, formal education, so their speech never improves. And then, when they grow into young adulthood, groups like the Taliban or other organized terrorists recruit them. Some become addicted to drugs, which inevitably leads to a life of crime. Many of these orphanages institutionalize the children they are supposed to look after.

Most NGOs that work with orphanages can provide donations that help to some extent, but many are also unethical. The funds that are supposed to support orphanages in underprivileged countries too often are "lost" during the transfer.

Nevertheless, most work energetically and diligently with good intentions. It is just that their positive impact is insufficient. In times when a nation suffers conflict and mayhem, all institutions can be devastated, so folks must protect themselves and those close to them before aiding orphans and the institutions that care for them.

Thus, even able family members who might otherwise be able to make a living are forced to become caretakers, taking on the stress of living in an unstable environment alongside the responsibility of caring for loved ones who have been physically or mentally pressed to the breaking point.

The government funds to support orphanages—from the assembly in the Walewale district of Ghana to the provincial government of Badakhshan, Afghanistan—is almost invariably menial. A child will often be better off staying with any relative compared to an orphanage, where the environment can be detrimental for the child.

One is bound to develop a strong mindset against wars when one witnesses parents losing their children, children losing parents, and kids being massacred for what they do not comprehend. Such experiences might make one feel powerless. It could make one feel guilty for doing nothing and neglect the political tone behind the war.

Due to war and other armed conflicts, many individuals do not have the power to fight against the massive corruption in their countries. From preschool to universities and job vacancies, corruption distorts development in all spheres. Thus, individuals in corruption-ridden places often grow tired of governance live in fear and uncertainty.

Everybody hopes for safer and healthier living conditions for themselves and their families. Decades pass, and people suffer. Whether it's Afghanistan or Côte d'Ivoire, the value of life in strife-torn countries is reprehensible. Such suffering is extensive and only begins with the physical wounds of war. During periods of active fighting, people die or suffer injuries every day. The wounded often have no health insurance, social security, or disability allowance. All they have is their savings if they are lucky enough to have any.

Otherwise, they must rely on whatever other income their family has. Further, with sparse and dismal medical facilities, the injured often have no option other than to have their families or other relatives take care of them. Such harsh conditions naturally inspire people to leave their home countries for better futures elsewhere.

Many leave as refugees and travel to other nations on perilous boats. Many seek tourist visas and declare themselves as refugees as soon as they reach the foreign land. And some simply start walking toward Europe or some other country, always hoping for a better life.

The feelings of helplessness these situations inspire, especially when combined with a strong compulsion to leave one's country, turn many individuals into prey for con artists and criminals who intend to organize scams rather than helping anyone beyond themselves. Known as 'scammers', such individuals seek to profit off of the suffering of others and stop at little to do so. Several illicit emigration agencies are active in most third-world countries. Often, they promise some kind of visa, if not a certificate of permanent residency, for a European and/or North American country. Such agencies may charge more than $10,000 for their counterfeit documents.

They might offer tourist and student visas. They complete applications for tourist visas after making bogus travel reservations and forging bank statements that confirm an ample amount. The agencies often deposit that temporarily to prove the applicant has enough currency for their holiday. But if the victim is stopped at immigration, they never get their money back and are simply turned away with nothing, made a victim to the scam and worse off than they started. Nevertheless, even with the knowledge of these traps being so common, desperation drives thousands to seek any path for escaping the atrocities of war.

Phony passports, ostensibly from high-income countries, sell for at least $30,000. Often, these are stolen passports the illicit agencies tamper with, utilizing graphic editing, so the picture resembles the persons buying the counterfeit forms. A hazardous albeit option is to book passage on a cargo ship or otherwise cross a border inside a cargo container.

Many people who chose this method have suffocated or died of thirst or starvation. What's more reprehensible is that the individuals signing on for such a venture may not realize the danger they're putting themselves in. The agencies responsible for all this illegal and inexcusable activity often market their services in terms of providing opportunities to study abroad, but they may work in partnership with unscrupulous shipping companies.

Many people seeking to escape war zones attempt to marry their cousins who have already left the country. This is an ordinary way of getting sponsorship. In these cases, the phony agencies arrange bogus marriages. Once the immigration authorities have approved the sponsorship, the person can travel to the country; then the couple no longer has to falsify the relationship. Although many try this method, the process can take months or even years. Immigration authorities scrutinize these applications close to determine whether the imminent marriage is genuine.

As an expatriate working in Ghana and Côte d'Ivoire, I sometimes encountered individuals who wanted to leave those countries and looked for agencies or ex-pats like me to help them. One person can only do so much, but there are ways to help without putting such individuals at the mercy of predatory agencies and scammers. If you ever find yourself in such circumstances, direct the individual to their government's website that handles immigration and visa applications. Those sites have everything to comprehend the process of legally emigrating or obtaining a student or tourist visa. Almost every national government has a website with extensive information, and while legal emigration may be a slow and sometimes frustrating process, it is far superior to being preyed upon by agencies such as those that sprung up to take advantage of desperate and hopeful emigrants.

Having an appropriate role model is another crucial factor in the development of a country. I spoke with a few folks in the Ghanaian village where I resided and realized that people often desire to imitate their more affluent neighbors. In essence, wealthy people became their role models without contemplating their source of income. They regard morals less, and they assume money is the ultimate source of respect. Consequently, corruption continues to be a serious impediment to progress.

Fig. 15 Border crossing of Kokul – Ai Khanoum between Afghanistan and Tajik istan. The only way to cross is on a decrepit ferry.

Fig. 16 Tajikistan immigration and customs at the Kokul – Ai Khanoum border crossing from Afghanistan.

Fig. 17 Border Crossing between Ghana and Burkina Faso. One can easily cross without any legal formalities if one is of Sub Saharan African ethnicity.

Fig. 18 Ghana- Burkina Faso border, to save custom duty on the import/export of bikes, the smugglers pay kids to ride it across the border one at a time. Since the locals don't require any visas or passport, hence they are able to transport the goods easily without paying the legal tariff.

Chapter 9.

Drug Addiction and General Health Care

Besides deaths and injuries, wars create significant tension and inflict adverse long-term health effects on thousands of people. Not all injuries can be treated by surgeons; victims of the war suffer grievously from psychic wounds that often go untreated.

I saw or met many people in Afghanistan who now have some chronic physical disability or mental disorder. Local soldiers who have been injured and subsequently discharged typically receive no significant psychiatric counseling. Even cash payouts to wounded soldiers and their families don't amount to much. All too often, corrupt officials take a cut from these government grants to the wounded. Of course, such practices further degrade trust in the government and the country's leadership, which only makes the Taliban recruitment effort easier.

Throughout conflict-torn and impoverished countries, shortages of adequate and timely medical assistance increase casualty totals. High rates of maternal and infant mortality reflect the stigma associated with having children out of wedlock and traditional birth practices that are unhygienic and medically unsupervised.

In Ghana and Côte d'Ivoire, it came to my attention that the culture around sex is far more liberal than in Afghanistan, in some respects. Many teenage girls with inadequate sex education end up pregnant. Wherever I went in Ghana, I came across young girls who had already become mothers. Plenty of them were migrant workers from rural villages, who are collectively known as *kayayei*. They work in various cities, and some, unfortunately, end up in prostitution due to there being few opportunities for them to earn an honest living. Of course, unwanted pregnancies are not the *only* outcome of inadequate sex education; sexually-transmitted disease is rampant in Sub-Saharan Africa.

As most of these cultures have taboos around STDs, people are reluctant to get tested. Those who do usually do so in a town far from their homes, which is where they can also get treatment, because such clinics are widely scattered, especially in rural areas. Making matters worse, there are witch doctors in Western Africa who have large followings in certain rural areas. These witch doctors tell patients that sex with virgins can cure HIV/AIDS, which, of course, is far from the truth.

Additionally, even though there is an increasing number of sex education programs in Sub-Saharan Africa, many people still do not take these lifesaving courses seriously. I had spoken to numerous youths while working at the University of Cocody in Côte d'Ivoire. The classes and series of interactions with students confirmed to me that many of these young people indulge in unprotected sex.

It was startling and worrisome. It appeared that these students had blatantly ignored the information that was provided to them by the university, which had mounted various campaigns to stress the importance of safe sex within its student population. When I had asked these young individuals why they chose to have unprotected sex, the students had different rationalizations. Some said that they trusted their partner to be honest and keep them safe from transmittable disease. Others told me that they simply couldn't find a condom during the moment.

On the other hand, any successful HIV/AIDS development programs in Afghanistan must be done with extreme caution, due to the conservative culture of the country. Candid information has to be softened, and hard facts must be censored for these programs to take place. In my personal experience, I never heard any organization candidly discuss the issue of HIV/AIDS or sex education, at least not openly. All issues and discussions surrounding HIV and safer sex precautions have to be targeted with extreme caution, and that caution often comes at the risk of holding back the complete facts that could save individuals from HIV infection.

Eradicating endemic and preventable disease continues to be a monumental task in Afghanistan. A prime reason for this is that many parents do not want their children to receive vaccines. Misinformed, they worry about physical harm associated with vaccination, and many believe that the United States promotes vaccinations nefariously with the intent of slowly poisoning or tracking the moments of the population.

After the news broke that medical workers who were providing polio vaccinations in rural Afghanistan and Pakistan informed the CIA of Osama bin Laden's residence, people began shunning vaccinations in large numbers. Many religious people also believe that receiving a vaccination is going against the will of God. Consequently, Afghanistan and Pakistan are the only countries on Earth today where polio still paralyzes or kills dozens every year.

Severe Pregnancy Risks

Even though women having children out of wedlock is much more common than it used to be, there is still a strong stigma attached to unmarried women who have children. The risk of maternal mortality is highest for girls under 15 years old, and complications in pregnancy and childbirth are higher among girls aged 10 to 19 than women aged 20 to 24. These adolescent girls usually take a pregnancy test only after the pregnancy is obvious; some are unaware of their pregnancies until the birth is almost imminent. Consequently, few receive adequate prenatal and postnatal care, jeopardizing not only the mothers' lives but also those of their babies.

In many African villages, women still have their babies delivered in the traditional way, which is culturally familiar to them, less expensive than seeking licensed medical care, and more convenient due to the sheer distance clinics tend to be from these rural parts.

During my visits to these far-spread clinics, I discovered that most of them are poorly supplied and poorly equipped. Even so, mothers and mothers-to-be received better care at clinics than the care they would receive back in their villages.

Traditional childbirth practices in African villages include home deliveries by typically untrained attendants or herbalists using home remedies, leading to greater cases of maternal and infant deaths. At least the clinics had trained medical attendants to assist during emergencies. To their credit, the Ghanaian and Ivorian governments have published messages encouraging people to use the clinics more often, but further convincing is needed throughout Sub-Saharan Africa and most low-income countries worldwide.

The stigma attached to teenage pregnancies and pregnancies out of wedlock drives many young women to get abortions, which unfortunately are easiest to get in unsafe places — again putting the lives of the young women at terrible risk. Some even use the services of so-called "black magic doctors," many of whom are native Nigerians, to "heal" their pregnancies. Of course, this only exacerbates the sad statistics on maternal and infant mortality.

The Added Risk of Malaria

Malaria is yet another reason for the high rates of maternal and infant mortality in Sub-Saharan Africa. Pregnancy reduces a woman's natural immunity against malaria, a deadly disease that also causes dangerous symptoms, including fever, chills, gastrointestinal distress, and severe anemia. Personally, I can attest to the severity of the illness as it takes shape in the healthy adult male. For the unborn child, maternal malaria increases the risk of spontaneous abortion, stillbirth, premature delivery, and low birth weight — a leading correlate with child mortality.

At the local hospital in Walewale, Ghana, I recall that a newborn or new mother died almost every day. I still remember the horror of hearing a new mother cry out in panic and desperation as she saw her child pass away — that's the kind of scene you can never wash out from your mind, no matter how hard you might try. I have watched new mothers collapse in shock after losing a newborn. At other times, a new mother's family would have to forcefully separate her from the motionless corpse of her baby.

The painful experience of being exposed to others' suffering is something that I can never forget.

In Afghanistan, the situation is largely the same. Many families insist on home births because rural clinics have so few female doctors and midwives. The conservative and patriarchal culture of Afghanistan also takes a dim view of allowing one's wife or daughter-in-law to be treated by a male doctor or midwife.

The consequent lack of facilities and medical expertise leads to unfortunate levels of maternal and infant mortality. The Afghan government, like those in Côte d'Ivoire and Ghana, encourages women to make use of the clinics, and one sees quite a few posters in streets and public places advocating safe motherhood. The government even provides free transportation to and from clinics, but the cultural bias against modern medicine and Afghanistan's low literacy rate have largely thwarted the government's efforts.

Child Disabilities and Deformities

The decades of war in Afghanistan have also left a legacy of children born with severe deformities. The medical reasons for this tragedy are varied. I learned that these deformities are frequently the result of ignorance and medical malpractice — the conservative culture has not helped this situation with its prohibitions against women seeing doctors or other medical professionals of the opposite sex.

The high prevalence of consanguineous marriages is also one of the attributes that contribute to congenital anomalies. In basic terms, it is a union between two individuals who are related as second cousins or closer. As per Cambridge University Press, the proportion of consanguineous marriages in Afghanistan is 46.2%.

Many of my colleagues and security guards were married to their cousins. Since bride price is high, many marry within their extended family to negotiate a lower payment, and also to ensure that the wealth remains within the family. Thence, children from consanguineous marriages are twice as likely to have genetic disorders as compared to non-related couples.

Multitudes of families don't have the resources to properly care for their child who is born with a severe disability, which may require medicines or adaptive therapies. Many Afghans believe that congenital disabilities are retribution for the sins of the child's parents. Consequently, these poor children are widely hidden from their communities to avoid bringing shame upon their families. Then, when they reach an employable age, most businesses would never consider hiring them.

Owners of such businesses even take pride in this form of discrimination because of their religious and cultural beliefs, which assert that the disabled deserved their impairments and attendant suffering as punishment for the evil deeds of their parents or that the children themselves supposedly committed in their past lives.

In many war-torn countries, some parents of disabled children go as far as to abandon their babies at the worst kinds of orphanages, institutions where the funding and staffing are much worse than at typical orphanages that struggle to provide the most basic necessities, such as sufficient food, for the children.

Due to a lack of expertise on the plentiful ways in which cognitive impairments can occur, any child with any form of cognitive impairment is treated the same as any other. This is a terrible fate for children whose disabilities are not profound. The capabilities they do possess are never fully developed, if developed at all, meaning that they suffer more than they would have ever had to had they received appropriate education and support. Society never gains the benefit of the contributions these individuals could have provided by shutting them away and scarcely acknowledging that they exist.

Also, many physical disabilities result from a lack of medical facilities. I know of a case like this concerning a boy from the village of Walewale, Ghana. He had fallen down the stairs of his school and broke his hand, but received no medical attention. As a result, his broken hand became permanently disabled. It could have been treated with a cast. I know of several hundred other cases in both Western Africa and Afghanistan in which minor injuries became permanent disabilities because the injuries were not given the routine treatment necessary for them to heal.

Behavioral Issues

Most children who grow up amidst armed conflict unsurprisingly tend to have trust and anger issues. Years of domestic instability have robbed these children of the normal care and attention that every child needs in order to mature into a socially acceptable adult who is unhindered by the very real effects of trauma sustained in youth.

Girls tend to be excessively shy and reserved; even groups of girls walking together on the streets tend to be much quieter than their counterparts in high-income countries. On the other hand, males tend to be about the same as they are everywhere: loud and mischievous. Armed conflict destroys the normal domestic certainties of society, leaving people unsure of whom they can trust and how much they can trust, even when dealing with friendly acquaintances.

Also, armed conflict almost always enhances casual access to firearms, so small arguments between men who have not learned to moderate their aggression can become deadly in a matter of seconds. Hence, everyone is vigilant for their own security and the security of their loved ones.

During my time in Ghana, I witnessed several physical assaults in the offices where I worked. Usually, it was the employer who physically assaulted a local employee. These employees, not the employer, were then terminated without any severance pay. Aside from the uncontrolled aggression of the employer, these unjustified incidents made me aware of the power imbalance in these offices and the wanting rights and protections of the employees.

Another consequence results from when a government's judiciary and police lose the trust of the people they should be serving: people take justice into their own hands. For example, residents of villages in Ghana and Côte d'Ivoire rarely call the police when an emergency occurs. Instead, they rely on their family and friends for urgent assistance. Actions are taken more effectively if the family is well-known, or if they are financially capable of bringing the issue to the media to shame the police. The bonds of personal networks also tend to be stronger in developing and conflict-torn countries. I think this comes from people being forced to address personal security issues informally through networks of friends and family when they cannot count on the police and other government security forces to protect them.

Rampant Drug Addiction

Another major health issue that afflicts Afghanistan is the abuse of illegal drugs. Drug addiction, along with its accompanying crime and mortality, affects nearly every country. It destroys healthy relationships and families all over the world. WHO considers drug addiction a complex disease that almost always requires treatment and healing — far more than good intentions or a strong will. Addictive drugs change the brain in ways that make quitting extremely difficult, even for those who sincerely desire to do so.

As the scene of war and mayhem for decades, Afghanistan has a population that has suffered tremendously. So, it is not surprising that many people seek emotional refuge in mind-altering drugs. During my field visits to rural Afghanistan, I met several people who were addicted to one drug or another.

Rates of drug addiction have been on the rise in Afghanistan, a sad statistic that reflects many societal failures, including a lack of legitimate employment opportunities for mainly younger Afghans, who consequently lose their hope for a better future.

Many returned refugees from other countries wash up in Afghanistan, too. You can see hundreds of them on the streets of Kabul using all kinds of drugs. Expatriate workers typically receive strict warnings from their employers against walking in certain neighborhoods of Kabul. In these areas, drug addicts are known to congregate, and some can be violent.

Every day, dozens of addicts die on Kabul's sidewalks without having received any assistance from the government. A few of these addicts are hardened criminals or even murderers (as a side note: many of their murder victims are people who have been accused of blasphemy). According to the National Center for Biotechnology Information (NCBI), the majority of addicts are 18 to 27 years old. Having no motivation to improve their lives and no families to support them, many join the Taliban or other insurgent groups, where they find a semblance of that support and a feeling of acceptance. That feeling of acceptance and having a cause to live for is what makes most of them join the Taliban.

There are medical professionals in most of the areas that I visited in Afghanistan and Sub-Saharan Africa. Still, the sad fact is that many more qualified medical practitioners have left the country for better opportunities and safety abroad. The remaining practitioners have mostly been treating war casualties, which can understandably take a heavy toll on their mental health. These are dedicated, brave, and highly honorable individuals who are serving their country to the best of their abilities. However, too often, these doctors and medical practitioners become addicted to drugs themselves to relieve the pain and stress of being such close witnesses to human suffering.

When I visited a drug rehabilitation center in Ishkashim in Badakhshan, Afghanistan, I came to realize that drug addiction requires far more attention than these centers are able to provide and that treatment facilities require significantly larger budgets to successfully rehabilitate patients.

If someone is identified as an addict by family members or friends in an Afghan village, they are referred to the district's rehabilitation center. In addition to extreme dependence on one or more drugs, symptoms of addiction include violent behavior and unresponsiveness.

Obviously, all of these realities can be stressful for the addict's family and friends. Once admitted to a center, the addict stays there for at least two weeks, essentially incarcerated except in the case of an emergency. Rehabilitation centers in rural areas of Badakhshan, Afghanistan, receive about 30 to 35 patients per month. Rates of successful rehabilitation vary depending on the center, but 60 percent seems to be an average rate.

Active fighting in a district inevitably results in reduced budgets at the centers, so many centers are unable to treat all of their patients during those periods. Fewer beds in rehabilitation centers lead to more families disowning their addicted sons (the substantial majority are men), making these young men extremely vulnerable to the call of the Taliban and other insurgent groups.

During my visit to the rehabilitation center, I was astonished to see that all of the patients were very calm, soft-spoken, and seemed to be motivated to end their addiction and rejoin their families and society. I was very interested to hear them speak frankly to me about their journey — how they first started using drugs and how their drug use worsened until they were unable to function at all without it.

One thing I heard repeatedly was that drugs provided them relaxation from everyday fieldwork in agriculture. Many used drugs to mask chronic pain and illnesses, to keep warm during cold weather, and to ease the psychological pain of unemployment. I also learned to my surprise that many became addicted because they had seen religious leaders (mullahs) using drugs. Even mothers, when faced with food shortages, would use drugs to relieve hunger, and some would also give these drugs to their babies and children to quell the same gnawing pain.

Patients told me that the most common challenge was limiting their intake of drugs during the first week, as this was when the cravings were the most intense. Withdrawal symptoms seemed to be about 80-percent psychological stress and about 20-percent physical pain. Although many were able to leave the center addiction-free, most would soon relapse because the government could not afford support programs for the unemployed. Among the patients, heroin was the most commonly used drug, followed by opium, crystal meth, hashish, and more.

The United Nations Office on Drugs and Crime (UNODC) estimates that Afghanistan produces about 90 percent of the world's opium and is the leading producer of hashish, and most of it finds its way to the illicit market. Opium farms are exceedingly common throughout Afghanistan. I saw many during my field visits.

The government has established essentially no hard restrictions against growing opium, as it is profitable not only for struggling farmers but also for the corrupt authorities who oversee its exportation to other countries. The Afghan government lacks the necessary funding, institutional capacity, and control mechanisms to guarantee the legality of their opium production and distribution. Those who cultivate and trade opium for legitimate medical uses compete directly with illegal traffickers. This drives up the price and consequently encourages increased cultivation. So, farmers who had been growing only legal crops turn to opium cultivation to meet the illegal market's demand. In the end, the total acreage of poppy cultivation increases steadily because of growing local and international demand.

Quite simply, it seems that almost any farmer would grow more poppies to supply the ever-growing crowd of purchasers.

Most donors to international development organizations have a profound interest in funding security and development projects such as in agriculture, education, and healthcare. But these organizations seldom fund drug rehabilitation centers, which desperately need attention, because drug addiction is a difficult and unattractive problem for them to work on.

Drug addiction fuels Taliban recruitment, yet Afghan rehabilitation centers cannot admit all of the addicts who are earnestly seeking treatment, leaving them to die on the streets or join any of the militia groups that are looking for more cannon fodder.

Who knows just how many innocent lives could have been spared, and invaluable lives saved, had the problem of drug addiction been handled more successfully?

The destructiveness of this issue reaches far beyond those who are addicted and the facilities that are endeavoring to help them recover. It is a systemic failure that will only worsen in the years to come if nothing is done to mitigate the root causes of drug addiction in Afghanistan.

Fig. 19 HIV wagon for free testing in rural Ghana. Stigma around HIV and AIDS still exists in most parts of the world.

Chapter 10.

Political Context

During my time living with the Afghan and African locales, I saw a string similarity that they were a lot more interested in local politics. This is mostly true for all the developing and conflict nations because the political policies have a greater impact on their livelihoods. The government sets prices and subsidies for essential items like flour, salt, and gasoline (with many other items being regulated), and this affects the majority of the population, especially when a large percentage is below the poverty line.

Similarly, profit margins of local businesses are already lower, with inflation or tax changes significantly affecting these businesses across the African continent. This puts peoples' already fragile livelihoods at risk. So, there are naturally compelled to pay attention to politics. When they observe that things are not going their way, the desperation leads to intense protests, which unfortunately, can turn violent.

Although Afghanistan and most countries in Western Africa are officially democracies, they still lack the kind of transparency necessary for minority voices to be at least heard, if not heeded. With support from UN agencies and well-meaning and well-funded NGOs, these countries have made strides toward free and fair elections and credible judiciary systems. Still, we have much work left to do.

In Uzbekistan, the government sees any opposition critic as a significant threat to the country's sovereignty. Consequently, opposition parties are effectively hamstrung when they try to mount campaigns or engage in public debate about government policies. I know of cases where members of the opposition suddenly disappeared or met their fates in untimely and unlikely accidents. In one incident in 2005 in Andijan, Uzbekistan, several hundred protesters against poverty were massacred by the Uzbek government. Major international news outlets reported this slaughter, but the government-controlled media within the country broadcast only brief statements regarding the crisis.

In its news bulletins, Uzbek State TV said "an armed group of criminals" had attacked the security forces in Andijan: "The bandits seized dozens of weapons and moved on to attack a correctional colony, setting some convicts free." Describing the rebels as "extremists," they claimed that nine people had been killed and 34 wounded during the clashes. The local radio station had reportedly been taken off the air.

Authorities also blocked foreign TV news channels, including CNN and the BBC News. Uzbek individuals and groups have very minimal platforms to express their opposition to government policies they believe to be ineffective or unjust. Several families whose members went missing or to prison for expressing their views against the government. Sometimes, the government will bring false charges of religious terrorism against individuals who oppose their policies, and those who wind up in prison are often tortured.

To a great extent, much of this is equally true for Tajikistan, where government executives have absolute authority over the general public. To succeed in any venture, one must first be on the good side of government officials. Even international organizations must have the government's complete support for their agendas if they expect to implement any development programs in Tajikistan. Any conflict or disagreement about an international organization's agenda or policies can lead to the government expelling the organization from the country.

However, I know of some cases where international news organizations exaggerated the severity of human rights abuses in Tajikistan. But across Central Asia, governmental transparency is generally very low.

From the way it appears to me, Afghanistan has more political freedom now than Tajikistan and Uzbekistan, when compared with my time staying in these countries from 2010-16. One of the few positive aspects of all the unrest in Afghanistan during this century is that people now realize they must speak up for their welfare if they hope to achieve lasting stability for themselves and their families. People must act when "law and order" are more like mayhem, and when they or their loved ones are suffering because of political or societal injustices.

In Afghanistan—but neither in Tajikistan nor Uzbekistan—I frequently saw people discussing politics in public. But these were Afghan citizens. I strongly advise all foreigners in Afghanistan against emulating this behavior. Doing so could put you at risk of being branded as a political agitator and possibly becoming a victim of violence. Politics is a sensitive topic, hence caution should be exercised.

To some extent, this is true in many countries. Locals often do not appreciate foreigners criticizing their politics. It can offend their patriotic feelings. I had similar experiences during my time in China, people did not appreciate foreigners criticizing the Chinese Communist Party's policies concerning Hong Kong, Taiwan, Tibet or Xinjiang to the local population of the People's Republic.

In Ghana and Côte d'Ivoire, people in small villages and large cities alike have more freedom to debate political issues openly, compared to Central Asian countries. Liberty is similar to many liberal countries—people sometimes openly debate in villages among their friends in public. This is encouraging development in Western Africa, as more people speak their opinions about political and social issues. People even organize political rallies in these countries, although, at times, I thought the free lunches provided by the organizers were a more prominent attraction than the political ideas on offer. I suppose they figured a bigger crowd is a better crowd, regardless of what caused them to gather.

In Ghana, political parties campaign by driving around the country in the days and weeks before an election, seeking public support. The typical entourage is very long, and sometimes the drivers are drunk. Several incidents in which inebriated campaign drivers were involved in collisions resulted in gruesome injuries and even death, sometimes to innocent young children. Typically, the party in power has the most campaign resources. So much so that they can pay supporters who are willing to campaign for them.

In developing and conflict-torn countries, corruption is often widespread. Evidence of this comes from the lifestyles of politicians who, during even short tenures in office, make millions of dollars. Such corruption can destroy a country's institutions.

To gain popular support, most political parties make promises that are, of course, never fulfilled. Once, just before election day in Ghana, one of the parties erected utility poles in many villages, hoping to indicate that they would bring electricity to those villages if they were voted into power. Similarly, some parties sponsor the preliminary construction of roads in some areas, hoping that the people will think the construction will continue to completion if they win in the election.

Naturally, none of these projects progress after election day, even when the sponsoring party wins. So, you wind up with villages bristling with utility poles connected to nothing and a few meters of the paved road here and there. As soon as the sponsoring political party is in power, their priorities shift toward self-dealing.

Sometimes, a party's electoral success hinges less on its political agenda than the amount of noise its campaign can make around town. They commission musicians to compose songs about their development plans and hire traditional dancers to make the songs more festive. Along with the free lunches and so on, all this entertainment does seem to cheer village populations, even if it's only for the days and weeks immediately preceding the elections.

A lot of this goes on in Côte d'Ivoire, too but with a French twist. The country was formerly a French colony and is still dependent on the French government in many respects. From my experience, the locals seem to feel that the French government has been responsible for several periods of unrest in the country.

Economically, the French government benefits from old and unfair trade agreements and land rights—the country exports many raw materials such as cocoa and rubber. These unfair agreements are in place only because the corrupt government in Côte d'Ivoire agreed to all these unfair trade agreements. During my time in Côte d'Ivoire, none of the Ivorian people I met supported or were favorably disposed toward the French government in any way. That hasn't stopped Paris, however, from maintaining its influence and authority over most Western African nations. Somehow, the Ivorian political parties that have the support of the French government always win worked. They would then be paid as international staff, earning considerably more than they would if they were citizens of that country.

The risks taken by the local staff are usually deadlier in areas that are under insurgencies. They are expected to take more field monitoring trips than international workers. This means that they are expected to represent the organization even when the Taliban or one of the other terrorist group is hostile to their organization. I recall in Afghanistan, many of our local staff often surveyed the districts of Warduj and Jurm, which were under the Taliban. They needed to ensure that those areas are serviced. It was a life-threatening task because the Taliban perceive most, if not all, development organizations as enemies. Yet, they had to do it.

Further, they cannot escape anywhere if they acted against their government and the government decides to take action against them. They are often considered enemies who are working for foreign governments by the Taliban. That is a mark that they cannot take off themselves, even when development missions in their area are over. Intuitively, the Taliban can come for them at any time. It is worse to imagine that the people in these categories are heavily underpaid, especially when compared to their international counterparts who are not exposed to such a level of risk.

Though, having foreign employees in positions of authority is crucial to have specialized capacities in underprivileged areas. Moreover, these foreigners are more likely to make decisions without fearing the repercussions from the host country's government with their diplomatic immunity. In contrast, local employees can easily be prosecuted by some governing bodies for taking decisions that are not in confluence with the government, especially if the host country has a high score on human rights violations.

Most governments claim that their decisions are in the best interests of their citizens. However, the reality is that they have influenced their media platforms to omit facts in their propaganda. With that, they can cover up the atrocities and activities that violate human rights. It happens in developed nations too.

The only way to get the facts is to tailgate news media from other countries. By way of illustration, the truth about Pakistan will not be heard in a Pakistani media platform because they are all censored. One should listen to Indian's reports on the Pakistani's activities, and vice versa. There are sometimes propaganda and slanders, but the facts are always decoded from each country's arguments and counterarguments.

Similarly, the damaging effects of western policies in Afghanistan and several African countries are not always portrayed by their international media. Apart from the government censors, many media and international organizations are after success stories. They do not get credible data that captures full realities, and, as such, they formulate their reports based on the policies presented to them. They miss the heartbreaking realities in the process. So, the best way to get the facts is to talk to the locals or follow the local media.

Many people protest the current political perceptions in Afghanistan, Tajikistan, and Uzbekistan. Many render their voice under anonymous Facebook accounts. It was clear that their lives would be at stake if they attempted to openly counter the community's political, cultural, and religious customs. Nevertheless, people make an effort to express their dissatisfaction behind the veil.

According to the United Nations Development Program, 86% of the world's resources are consumed by the wealthiest 20% in the world. The remaining 80% of the world's population have to grapple 14% between themselves. This misallocation is the reason many people toil all their lives in less developed nations. Despite working from Mondays to Sundays, many street vendors, shop owners, and other small businesses live an unreasonably low quality of life. They eventually resort to crimes and illegal means since there are no assurances that they will succeed if they remain on the proper path. They evade taxes and exploit one another.

There was a particular situation that I witnessed in Walewale, Ghana. The price of gas was expected to shoot up in a few days, and a few locals tried to buy all the fuel available in the local gas stations. They hoarded the fuel, so none was available locally. It would have to be purchased at a higher price from those who hoarded it. This was a black market, an illegal business, and it is proof of how desperate the people have become in a bid to make a living.

In an environment where political instability, civil conflicts, and intense poverty are tearing the people apart, social themes like gender and human rights are not paid serious attention. The focus is on pressing projects like health, agriculture, or peace and stabilization projects. Gender and human rights activism can be developed when life-threatening circumstances are fixed. After all, it is impossible to develop social or infrastructural features when necessary peace and security are not guaranteed. For example, a hospital may take a government or international agency years to build. But it can be blown up in a minute by rocket fire.

Similarly, due to ongoing military conflicts and massive shortages of basic necessities, the practice of protecting the environment does not hold much water to the people. I saw massive usage and poor disposal of plastic all over Afghanistan and West Africa, which is eventually a disaster for nature. The concept of recycling is still taken with a pinch of salt because people are concerned about the survival of their families and themselves. Thusly, environmentally friendly practices will never be taken seriously until basic livelihood, peace, and security are guaranteed.

Fig. 20 Political Campaign in Walewale, Ghana

Fig. 21 Chiefs of Walewale, Ghana at a local ceremony

Fig. 22 Walewale, Ghana- utility poles in villages connected to nothing.

Fig. 23 Staff on monitoring visits- Badakhshan, Afghanistan

Fig. 24 Development Staff conducting field monitoring visits through dangerous routes in Afghanistan.

Chapter 11.

The Taliban

In 1994, the Taliban emerged as one of the prominent factions in the Afghan Civil War. Students from the Pashtun areas of eastern and southern Afghanistan who had been educated in the madrassas and who fought during the Soviet-Afghan War filled their ranks at that time. They fought back against the Soviet occupiers and bogged them down in viscous a-symmetrical guerrilla warfare.

However, after the Soviets withdrew from Afghanistan and the USSR collapsed, what was left was a well-armed radical group of militants without an occupying force to fight against. These militants emerged as the Taliban and a prominent faction in the following Afghan Civil War. Ironically, they were the same soldiers that the U.S. government had supported in their fight against the Soviets.

In a textbook case of blow-back, the group, the Americans had originally funded began a campaign of terrorism and radical indoctrination. This group has terrorized the world with inhumane and savage ideologies and practices. They are one of, if not the, most hated groups of political militants in the world. The Taliban (which means "students" in Pashto) refer to themselves as the Islamic Emirate of Afghanistan. In the name of their own violent interpretation of Sunni fundamentalism, they have orchestrated numerous atrocities in Afghanistan and across the world since their inception over the past two and a half decades.

From 1996 to 2001, the Taliban held power over roughly three-quarters of Afghanistan, ruling according to a strict interpretation of Sharia law. During that time, only Pakistan, the UAE, and Saudi Arabia recognized their government. The governments of many other countries have since condemned those governments for recognizing the Taliban.

The Taliban's harsh enforcement of their interpretation of Sharia law has resulted in the brutal treatment of many Afghans, especially women, and has earned the group worldwide condemnation. Even now, Afghan women have a very harsh life, but during the Taliban era, the situation was much worse. Abuses were myriad and violently enforced by the religious police.

For example, the Taliban issued edicts forbidding women's education, forcing girls to leave schools and colleges. Women who ventured out of their homes were required to be accompanied by a Maharam and were obliged to wear the burqa. Those accused of disobeying these edicts were publicly beaten.

Today, the Taliban still controls about 40 to 50 percent of the country (down from about 70 percent from 1996 to 2001), and law enforcement in several provinces is still much as it was during Taliban rule. Unfortunately, the years of Sharia restrictions have turned certain enforced behavior into a habit. For instance, in the areas where the wearing of the burqa and hijab is no longer legally mandatory, societal norms now demand that women continue to dress in this attire when out in public.

After living and working with Afghans, I gained a deep understanding of how those on the ground felt about this geopolitical situation. Far from the desks of the United Nations, Pentagon, and White House, these people live with the repercussions of the decisions made by these far off institutions every day. When I spoke to various Afghans about their life under the Taliban, many indicated at it was a kind of life in hell.

Most of them are against the Taliban rule and strongly condemn the barbaric acts they committed. Many also feel betrayed by the American government, which they consider primarily responsible for the current and miserable state of their country. They feel that U.S. policies have failed on many fronts: drug addiction has increased, violence is still rampant, and the security situation continues to deteriorate even as billions of dollars have been spent in failed reforms of security and development initiatives.

Many are now seeing the Soviets in a more flattering light, realizing that they would have developed the country much better than the Americans have so far. This belief is only reinforced when Afghans juxtapose their state of affairs with the economies and infrastructure of other Central Asian former Soviet Republics like Tajikistan and Uzbekistan.

Reports show that since 2004, American drone attacks have killed only two percent of high-value targets in Afghanistan. In other words, most of the fatalities in these attacks have been innocent bystanders. Afghans, obviously, are aware of this, and because so many have lost family and friends to these attacks, they have far less faith in the American government than they once did.

Badakhshan is an Afghan province and one of the areas that were never entirely under the control of the Taliban (the Taliban did, however, gain control over several districts within the province). Badakhshan's capital is Fayzabad, where I lived for almost three years, and during that time, the Taliban never controlled the city.

While I was living in Fayzabad, a district about 50 kilometers (about 31 miles) distant, Baharak fell to the Taliban. When news of the fall of Baharak reached Fayzabad, I saw scenes of major panic and fear in the capital city. This victory for the Taliban seemed to indicate that their next target would be Fayzabad. Their victory here would certainly involve the killing of all persons who worked with government agencies and international organizations.

If the Taliban took over a territory, the only way an "infidel" was safe from murder was if only exceptions would have been high-profile individuals, who could be held for ransom. As soon as night fell, Badakhshan's governor left the city for Tajikistan, along with most other high-profile government officers. I and my foreign colleagues who worked for international organizations were left in a panic and a feeling of helplessness, not knowing whether our lives were about to be cut short.

In such a situation, escape via automobile or truck is by no means a sure thing, as surrounding districts could be under enemy control. At every security checkpoint, you risk capture when you don't know which side controls the checkpoint. So, the surest way to flee to safety is on an aircraft. I recall that our operations and security department had discussed or actually bought some burqas for men to disguise themselves in should we have to evacuate by land.

The environment was very tense, and I remember hearing of numerous negotiations within the U.N. agencies. Being under the threat of a hostile Taliban takeover of our city, we had to leave our residential compound. Most residents in the city knew where the residential compound of the international workers was, and we had to ensure we were not there in case there was any sort of violence. There was a day we had to vacate our residence to the house of our local Afghan colleague, just so we would be safe in case they eventually attacked.

Finally, after two days, the U.N. arranged some 30 to 40 flights by fixed-wing and helicopter aircraft to evacuate hundreds of people from Fayzabad. In a typical week, we would typically have only two or three flights. This was a narrow escape, even though the Afghan military was able to stop the Taliban at the outskirts of Fayzabad.

Afghanistan's reputation has undoubtedly suffered because of its associations with terrorism. The chaotic entropy that accompanies civil war has led Afghanistan to become a breeding ground for all types of militant and extremist groups. Not only is it a hotspot for Taliban militias fighting the Afghan government and NATO, but it also is a training area for many terrorist groups that operate all over the world. Aside from the Taliban, other terrorist groups operating in Afghanistan include Al-Qaeda, Lashkar-e-Omar, Lashkar-e-Omar, ISIS, etc., have all established a beachhead in Afghanistan. All high-profile terrorists have at some time, or others received training in Afghanistan.

Members of these terrorist organizations enter Afghanistan from Pakistan to the east and south, China to the northeast, Iran to the west, and Turkmenistan, Uzbekistan, and Tajikistan to the north. Most of these individuals come from Pakistan, but the most brutal and barbaric ones come from Uzbekistan to train in Afghan camps. Some of them are a part of the Uzbekistan opposition and/or are members of the Islamic Movement of Uzbekistan. Militants also come to train in Afghanistan from Chechnya, Tajikistan, Egypt, Xinjiang (the "autonomous" territory in Northwestern China, home of the oppressed Uyghurs), and many high-income countries as well. In Taliban-controlled areas, small children receive lessons in hating the West and sacrificing themselves for Islam as an act of ultimate martyrdom.

The militants who come to Afghanistan from Xinjiang claim to represent the majority-Muslim Turkic (as opposed to ethnic Chinese) population of that territory. Xinjiang is where the "re-education" camps of Uyghur Muslims are taking place. These people have been fighting for independence from the rest of China. Unfortunately, this has caused many terrorist attacks in that territory. In retaliation, the Chinese government has taken an uncompromising stand against growing religious extremism in that region, and many consider this as stronger Chinese repression.

Both Uzbekistan and Tajikistan governments have made strong and successful attempts to minimize religious extremism in their respective countries. In this, they have received strong support from the Russian government, which wants to stop terrorists from coming to Russia from Afghanistan. With their rural and porous borders, the two nations are very vulnerable to the threat of spreading religious-extremist terrorism, much of which is funded by various groups and individuals from Saudi Arabia. They must continue taking the strong measures they have implemented to stop the influence of radical and religious extremism from spreading.

Foreign governments have accused those of Uzbekistan and Tajikistan of human rights violations. However, when it comes to regulating the religious thinking and preserving the country's secularism, the Uzbeks and Tajiks have been successful on many fronts due to the strong cultural influence of and financial support from Russia, aid which dates back to the Soviet Era. At Afghanistan's borders with Tajikistan and Uzbekistan, a heavy presence of border-patrol officers has been trained to shoot at anyone who looks as if they might enter the country without authorization.

During my stay in Badakhshan, the Taliban maintained a strong presence in the districts of Warduj and Jurm. They operated and conducted practically all their planning in Badakhshan from these districts. There were a constant ebb and flow of Taliban control of other districts in Afghanistan, over which they would occasionally take control until government troops would drive them out. Unfortunately, the Taliban is present in every province of the country, and every district has people who support the Taliban ideology and sympathize with them.

Many small criminal gangs also use the name of the Taliban to frighten the law-abiding populations where they operate. Some have been involved in kidnappings. Including these gangs, the number of Taliban in Afghanistan seems to be between 60,000 and 80,000, but the country's mountainous geography helps them conceal their whereabouts in caves and various other hideouts. Their number is very minimal compared to the Afghan and NATO forces, but they use guerilla warfare tactics, which are consistently identified as a means for less powerful actors to counter much stronger fighting forces. But imagining guerilla warfare as a "primitive'" weapon of the weak underestimates the complexity involved in fighting guerrilla wars. They often ambush, inflict damage, and disappear.

Many of the elder Taliban joined the movement in the late 1980s, and early 1990's when the CIA trained them against the Soviets. Although they have tactically adapted since then, they still rely on military training to project force and respond to battlefield developments. Many militants from Pakistan also train in Afghanistan, although their agenda involves attacks on India in the ongoing conflict in Kashmir.

In addition, the Haqqani network and the Pakistani Lashkar-e-Taiba terrorist organizations also have a strong presence in Afghanistan. Those organizations target Indians and are responsible for several terrorist attacks in India. Incidents have also occurred when the terrorist groups target non-Muslim Indians, often by checking to see if the kidnapped individual is circumcised. An uncircumcised person is not Muslim, and therefore, they are treated more harshly either with death or ransom. This terribly degrading practice was previously utilized in World War II by the Nazis to identify Jewish people. The Pakistani Taliban often do this to identify Indian Hindus in Afghanistan. Even though Indian Hindus and Pakistanis speak the same language and look similar, circumcision gives all away.

The Indian embassy and several of its 24 consulates in Afghanistan have been attacked several times. Pakistan's government has a similarly expansive presence in Afghanistan. As many Afghans know, both the ISI and RAW intelligence agencies are active and working towards the best interests of their respective countries in Southern Afghanistan. Similarly, former SVR and CIA are also present in Northern Afghanistan, as that part of the country borders several Central Asian countries that used to be parts of the Soviet Union.

Their typical modus operandi is to attack one village at a time, capture it, and then attack another nearby village until they have taken control over an entire district, again relying on guerilla attacks. Taliban forces will often try to capture hotels, as they are filled with potential hostages. They do the same with government buildings.

During ANSF or NATO airstrikes, the Taliban will use innocent civilians and kidnapped foreigners as human shields by holding them hostage in their hideouts. They use them as bargaining chips in their negotiations, which mainly involve demands for either financial resources or the release of captured Taliban soldiers. Because of this unfortunate practice, many innocent people have been killed in those airstrikes.

Whenever the Taliban takes over a hotel or other facility, they typically do so to strengthen their hand in negotiations with the government. They want the government to release Taliban prisoners or pay a ransom for high-profile hostages that they have captured. Sometimes, some of the Taliban fighters disguised as captured guests in a hotel. These methods have, at times, worked well for the Taliban. The government has, succumbed to Taliban pressure by releasing high-level members that they had captured and imprisoned on several occasion.

Not surprisingly, after these captured Taliban leaders were reunited with their cohort, they planned and carried out attacks more deadly than the ones they launched before. So, when negotiations lead to the government either paying a ransom or releasing deadly criminals, it is always a step back.

Consequently, whenever the Taliban or another terrorist group captures a hotel or other facility, the government and/or NATO forces now simply retaliate at the location to regain control, all without regard to the safety of the captives. The longer they allow the terrorist groups to control such sites, the more the media goes on about the hostages—which, of course only increases the difficulty of rescue missions.

Negotiations begin with less and less frequency because agreeing to negotiate implies the possibility of losing at the bargaining table. During these retaliatory attacks against terrorist groups, ANSF and/or NATO forces try to remove the terrorists from the facility as soon as they can, even if that means risking the lives of hostages. So, if you ever are unfortunate enough to be stuck in a facility that the Taliban or other terrorists capture, your chances of making it out safely are bleak.

After a typical rescue/retaliatory mission, the authorities inevitably say that all hostage deaths were at the hands of the Taliban. In a sense, this is always true (the deaths would not have occurred if the Taliban had not taken the hotel or whatever). But the bullets that cause hostage deaths come from the guns of ANSF and/or NATO troops more often than we care to imagine when the object is to defeat the terrorists at any cost. Many hostages die in the crossfire of these situations, whether by the Taliban or NATO.

Another reason why negotiations with the Taliban have decreased in recent years is that granting any concession to the Taliban—be it ransom for a hostage or releasing a Taliban prisoner—only encourages the Taliban to repeat their outrage. And not only the Taliban: common criminals pay attention to government practices too. Some gangs have kidnapped people and then sold them to the Taliban, knowing that the Taliban are likely to profit when the hostages are released.

When carrying out suicide bombing attacks, the Taliban often disguise themselves as government workers. Most attacks on government buildings were carried out by Taliban who were clean-shaven, dressed in a suit and tie, and carrying a small attaché case. Some Taliban are university educated and fluent in English, making it much harder to identify them in a bustling crowd.

The Taliban also heavily favor the use of suicide bombing and IEDs (improvised explosive devices). They have been one of the main causes of casualties in Afghanistan. They will simply hide an IED in a briefcase, walk into a government building or university and detonate their suicide bomb. Political transitions seem to cause drastic increases in violence and casualties. The insurgents are extremely anti-democratic and want Taliban rule all over the country. These attacks usually occur on Fridays, as Friday is the holiest day of the week in the Muslim calendar.

NGOs and International organizations always ensure that their vehicles do not look similar to military or government vehicles. It is one way they can ensure that they do not become targets to the Taliban in Afghanistan, who love to target the military or government's vehicles.

These terrorist organizations often have a handful of followers and members. They are only dangerous because they are heavily armed, and they are willing to waste themselves. This explains why they fearlessly take part in suicide attacks.

Radicalization preys on destitution. In recent years, the Taliban have been especially successful at recruiting new fighters, and their number will undoubtedly continue to grow with rising poverty and failed development policies. People in rural areas of several districts hardly have enough food to survive. They are extremely helpless, and if the Afghan government and/or international agencies don't provide them with any assistance, they become increasingly vulnerable to Taliban recruiting.

This is because the Taliban give them at least enough food to prevent their children from starving to death. The Taliban pays somewhere $500 and $1,000 as a bonus to recruits, while ANSF pays less than $200 per month. Many people in developed countries don't realize that ideology and religious beliefs often have little to do with a person's decision to join a terrorist organization. Quite frequently, joining the terrorists is simply a matter of earning a living in a time when one's options are few.

The Afghan war has taken an unknown number of innocent lives—young children and babies who were, presumably by accident, targeted by ANSF or NATO forces. Bunk intelligence and botched drone strikes have destroyed schools, hospitals, and homes of people who have no dog in this fight. Tragedies like these, and others, in which people who had nothing to do with any insurgent group lose their loved ones cause those people to also lose all hope and trust in their government and the foreign governments who are allied with theirs. Many people join the Taliban and become radicalized to avenge their loved ones killed by the supposed "good guys."

In such a state of desperation, fighting for the Taliban gives them new hope and aspirations of martyrdom. For many Afghans, the years of failed negotiations have given only false hope. So, unless development policies don't give Afghans enough resources now and enough to develop honest and sustainable livelihoods over the long haul, the Afghan/NATO coalition will continue to chase its own tail, and the Taliban will continue to simmer if not boil over.

In Côte d'Ivoire, the situation is similar. Practically none of the population wants conflict, and none are fighting for religious reasons. Yet continuing to see their country's natural resources pillaged by the industrialized nations and seeing their politicians live lavishly off kickbacks while the rest are struggling every day to provide for themselves and their family leads them to dissent.

After years of peaceful protests falling on deaf ears, these protests are turning into civil wars, which creates fertile soil for the seeds of extremism. None of the people I ever met in Africa was in favor of enacting and enforcing religious laws in their country. Practically all, however, demand credibility and transparency from their political systems.

Of course, NATO soldiers and foreign development workers have also been killed during the many years of war in Afghanistan. In certain instances, they are taken hostage, and their bodies can be found horribly tortured and mutilated - or not found at all. Neither are children spared; the Taliban will purposely kill children and babies, which understandably causes the Afghan people to want vengeance. Unfortunately, this eye-for-an-eye mentality creates a positive feedback loop of inhumanity, leading to the normalization of torturing captives by both sides.

Outside of murder and torture, the Taliban has also been waging a culture war. They have destroyed a lot of assets and resources, including the famous monumental statue of Buddha of Bamyan in 2001. This savagery doubles as a geopolitical information war as many in the West come to think of all Afghans as violent, intolerant, and backward. The rest of the world simply assumes that Afghans are insensitive and intolerant towards other people's religions. The sad part is that the Afghan people themselves are the ones most devastated by the Taliban.

The members of these terrorist groups like to see themselves as heroes. It is just the same way foreign soldiers are seen as heroes in their home country. The excitement of being a hero, a martyr for their country and religion is another odd reason that many people join these terrorist organizations. They have grown frustrated by years of war, and this is what the extremist exploits to recruit them. They make them fantasize about a better life after death, which requires them to die as martyrs first.

Taliban are infamous for the ruthless and fierce ways they attack people. In 2014, they killed more than 130 children in Peshawar, Pakistan, in an Army Public School. That incident devastated all religions and ethnic communities in Afghanistan and Pakistan. Parents, too, became extremely conscious of their children's safety in school. Schools also began to hire armed security afterwards. Such incidents are the fundamental reasons people hate terrorist organizations.

Every Afghan and Pakistani that I met expressed outrage when the Taliban are mentioned. The same outrage is expressed in West Africa at the mention of Boko Haram. Unfortunately, the constant massacre is why terrorist organizations are unpredictable. They can lay ambush attacks on civilians. They also disrupt education programs, and as such, international organizations must be tactful about setting up schools in Taliban dominated communities. They also have to make sure that their curriculum does not appear pro-west to the locals.

Within Afghanistan, many live in fear of religious leaders or other extremists. Consequently, they eventually come around to supporting a religious lifestyle. In addition, most of the Afghan media, reflecting substantially large financial investments from Wahhabi groups in Saudi Arabia, create a strong religious environment. This begins with programming for young children in which they incessantly hear the message that Sunni Islam is the only religion to follow if you want to go to heaven.

The growth of religious zealotry has also affected all the musicians and artists in the country. Afghan artists who stray from the straight and narrow are often a target for the Taliban and so must perform in secret. Religious extremists have attacked many concerts, causing countless musicians to flee the country for Tajikistan, where they can perform in safety. Afghan religious groups and the Taliban consider both music and dance as haram; oddly, one can easily find videos in which members of these terrorist groups are dancing with crossdressers or young boys.

Afghanistan has a unique culture of literature and music. Their poetry is enchanting, and their literary culture remains one of the oldest and most exciting in the world. Sadly, their literature and music are mostly showcased by the Afghan diaspora living abroad only. Several decades of conflict have taken their social life out of them.

Most of the refugees from the Afghan wars know the importance of freedom, and few would ever advocate for religion as a way of life or impose religious obligations on others.

While the news and media platform portray Afghanistan as a community with an avid interest in aggression and violence, this is not near the reality. The country is in crisis for decades, unquestionably. But most people do not desire conflicts. This is not different from what I experienced in West Africa.

Most people have an ordinary life in Afghanistan and the African countries I worked in. Parents put high hopes on the future of their children. They try to get the kids educated in the belief that they would live to their potential and build a stable future. Whether in Africa or Afghanistan, everyone I met has an intense hatred for terrorism. They express profound pains and intense disgust when they hear about the death of a person, regardless of such person's cultural, religious, and ethnic backgrounds. They see terrorism as a catastrophe within their countries. They just want the violence to end.

Fig. 25 Military guarding a local school in Afghanistan after attack on Army Public School in Peshawar, Pakistan

Fig. 26 Walewale, Ghana open market

Fig. 27 Zayaa Mosque-Shrine in Wulugu, Ghana made of mud–A hidden gem

Fig. 28 The Basilica of Our Lady of Peace of Yamoussoukro, Cote d'Ivoire. The largest church in the world. Gorgeous and stunning site.

Chapter 12.

Close Encounters, Cultural Shocks, and Lessons Learned

Overdosing on Paracetamol

During 2013, I was serving in Walewale, Ghana, when I experienced another, more personal crisis. On this particular day, I had been out completing my service, and I ate lunch at one of the street vendors. When I returned home that evening, I began to focus on how ill I felt. The combination of nausea and stomach pains initially made me think that I was suffering from food poisoning, and that seemed likely at the time as I had eaten somewhere that was entirely unfamiliar. I took my temperature to check and found that I was running a low-grade fever.

My next decision was based on a life-long avoidance of medications unless it was absolutely essential. I've always had a nagging feeling that getting comfortable with medication would lead to a loss of some form of control as I became increasingly dependent on chemical medications. It was why I had always avoided alcohol, smoking, or any form of recreational drugs.

This aversion also meant that I had refused other forms of medication, including the anti-malaria tablets recommended by health organizations when stationed in locations where malaria was a threat. I thought that I would be able to build up my immunity by simply continuing to live a healthy lifestyle.

Unfortunately, eating right and exercise are not effective against parasites like Plasmodium, which causes malaria. After that initial feeling of illness, I finally asked a local colleague to take me to the Walewale hospital.

He took me on his bike to the local hospital. By this point, I had a high fever, so I wasn't even able to walk, and my friend supported my every step. It is impossible not to muse over the extreme decline between that time and just a month before then, when I ran the Ghana International Marathon, finishing 43 Km in 35 degrees Celsius. Now, I was struggling to remain standing. It was a harsh reminder of just how quickly life can drastically change.

At the time, the Walewale hospital was the only big hospital for the entire village with one recognized doctor. The rest of the staff were medical assistants. As a foreigner, I was always made to be the priority when I needed to see a doctor, but not on this day. No, the only doctor was not at the hospital. As my colleague arranged for me to see a medical assistant, I felt just happy that I was going to receive any medical attention; I had never felt so physically drained in my entire life, either before or since then.

With a quick look at me and seeing my deteriorating condition, the medical assistant knew that I needed urgent care and prioritized me accordingly. He diagnosed me with malaria. Absolutely stunned, I could not mentally accept that diagnosis; I had learned that medical people in African villages are too quick to identify your condition as malaria, even without getting a blood test. I figured there were so many other things that it could be, including the flu.

However, I was in no state to dispute the diagnosis — I was so relieved to be receiving medical attention that I wasn't going to verbalize any apprehension or doubt that I had. The medical assistant gave my colleague a prescription, and he immediately filled the prescription at the hospital pharmacy. According to the prescription, I was to take four malaria tablets three times a day, and one tablet of paracetamol twice a day. This dosage was directed for the next three days. With a solution in hand, my colleague assisted me onto his motorbike for what felt like an incredibly long ride home. I had to stop him a few times as I was so sick that I had to vomit on the side of the street. We finally reached my house, and my colleague left me with some food and bottles of quinine drink recommended for people who have malaria.

That night, I ate a bit of food and fell into a fitful slumber. The next day, I begrudgingly ate breakfast and decided to take the medication as I still felt unwell. The prescriptions came in two small paper bags. One bag was labeled paracetamol with the directions of twice daily. The other bag was labeled malaria tablets with the directions of four tablets three times a day. Following these instructions, I waited for some hint that they were working. Any kind of alleviation would have been welcome, considering how I felt no better than the previous day. There was no discernible change, so I decided to remain in bed until I felt better. After dozing on and off for more than four hours, I rose to have a small lunch. I quickly attributed my dizziness and lack of appetite to malaria. In an effort to heal faster, I forced myself to eat and took the second dose of the day as prescribed: the second paracetamol and four more tablets.

This second dose was followed by a sense of drowsiness and confusion that meant I would need to remain in bed. I again dozed for most of the afternoon, waking around 5:00 PM. Noticing the time, I knew that I had to take the last dose of the day, and pulled myself up from the bed. After swallowing the pills, my stomach ache intensified, causing me to double over in pain for a few moments. In greater pain, I decided to look at the malaria medication for some hint of why I was feeling worse.

The problem was immediately apparent. The bag that was labeled paracetamol was actually the malaria tablets according to the bottle within the bag, the medication that should have been taken four times a day.

Shocked, I looked in the other bag and found that the bag marked as malaria tablets were actually the paracetamol, which was only meant to be taken twice a day. I had taken 12 paracetamols within an eight-hour span. I immediately began panicking about the risks of kidney, liver failure, or any other unknown side effects that could result from overdosing on paracetamol.

Even though I was so weak that I found it difficult to stand, I placed a direct call to the only doctor in Walewale. I explained the situation to him, emphasizing that I had taken well over the recommended dose for paracetamol. He ordered me to drink as much water as I could, then come to the hospital as soon as possible. Once I hung up, I began drinking water while calling my colleague to see if he would be able to provide me with another ride to the hospital. He reached my door within minutes.

I remember little about the ride as worry and illness battled over my focus, making the entire ride a blank in my memory. Once at the hospital, we hurried to the doctor's room. Ushering me over to a seat, he explained that he had already ordered banku (a local dish made of fermented corn and cassava) with some meat dish. While waiting for the food, he made sure that I continued to drink water and reminded me to keep drinking for the next few hours. Water was one of the best ways to flush the excess paracetamol out of my system. So, I sat in his office eating and drinking as much as I could with a stomach that was already upset, feeling miserable but hopeful. After an hour, the doctor examined me and determined that I was out of danger. He gave me permission to return home under the understanding that I was to call him if any other problems arose.

My colleague took me back to the house, but this time he stuck around to ensure that I ate and drank based on the doctor's recommendation. By that point, I was feeling a lot better; even the ailment that had driven me to the hospital in the first place had largely abated, so I was much more attentive than I had been in several days. After a couple of hours, the doctor called to make sure I was okay and verify that I continued to eat and drink regularly. After a heavy meal and the high stress from the day's events, I finally managed to get a good night's sleep for the first time in days. Though, in the back of my mind, there was a nagging doubt about my health.

The next day was like a miracle — I felt completely better, with only the memories as a reminder of just how difficult the last few days had been. Accompanied by my colleague, I went to the pharmacy that had given me the mislabeled medication. I spoke to the nurse who had given me the medication, explaining the wrong packets and how deadly this could have been for me. She was incredibly apologetic, explaining that her own exhaustion had likely contributed to this mistake — she had to prepare hundreds of medicine packets every day.

This kind of error would have resulted in the nurse being fired had it happened in a developed nation. But in Ghana, it was a daily occurrence. My own experiences had already taught me just how challenging it was to find skilled and qualified people for positions in the villages. Most of the educated Ghanaians move to bigger cities, leaving the more rural areas nearly devoid of people with the right skills for the most fundamental positions. I escaped a medical fatality, but I realized that African villages struggle in finding literate people and lacked the budget to train staff properly. These shortcomings frequently lead to medical negligence, the fact that I had gained an understanding of to some degree years earlier, while in Côte d'Ivoire.

Medical negligence in rural areas of developing nations (as well as nations in conflict) has resulted in an unknown number of deaths. Unfortunately, most of these cases of negligence go unreported because there aren't the necessary procedures in place to file reports. This is true even in rural Africa, where European and North American people are treating patients. At one point, an inquiry was initiated, and it determined that these so-called medical professionals had all faked their qualifications. They had exploited the extreme shortage of medical staff, especially in rural areas, where poor Africans are desperate to receive medical treatment from anybody claiming expertise. Negligence is a systemic problem, in large part because there are simply too few qualified doctors, both from the nation and outside help. The long hours can further impair the ability of a qualified medical professional as their decision making is impaired by exhaustion.

Studies show that people of European and North American descent are highly respected and thought of as literate people; hence, Africans are much more vulnerable to being deceived by them. To complicate matters, medical assistants do not receive regular training to update their skill set. Coupled with a lack of performance assessments and audits, chronic acts of medical negligence are perpetuated instead of being addressed and properly resolved.

Following my time in Ghana, I learned my lesson: When you receive a prescription from a doctor, always double-check the medication with a simple search online. Self-education is essential (not just something people do to second-guess their medical professionals). One should know the prescribed medication and its side effects. A simple search can fill in the gaps in your knowledge and significantly reduce the risks of living in a system that is stretched far too thin. The overprescribing or wrong prescription of drugs is not something uncommon in developing nations.

My own experience made me far more aware of what others in the nation must experience. For example, while eating at one of the popular village restaurants in Walewale, I met a friendly man, and we chatted as we ate. As what usually happens in these kinds of introductory situations, we casually discussed several topics. This led to a discussion about our families, and he mentioned that his wife had passed away recently. Surprised, I quickly offered sympathies and asked if he was able to talk about what had happened to her.

To my horror, he said she had overdosed on malaria tablets and died as a result. This time, the problem was medical negligence, at least not in the way I had experienced. The doctor had prescribed her proper dosage of tablets, making it clear what the recommended doses were, but she had heard that if she consumed them all at once, she would recover faster. After all, she had children to raise; she didn't feel that she could take a few days to heal.

Having taken the full pill bottle, she began to choke, then died within minutes. It was a tragic and heartbreaking story that is not only found in developing nations. This kind of thing can happen anywhere when people don't have even a basic understanding of how medicine works. It is one more thing that medical professionals need to do; explain that medicine has to be processed a little at a time in the body and that there is no quick fix.

Most illnesses cannot be cured with a simple pill or tablet. While it is not specific to developing nations, this kind of tragedy is more common where there is less access to general knowledge. The man even said that he had heard of several other incidents where extra doses were taken with disastrous results.

Hospital Negligence

In 2009, during my term in Abidjan, I worked at a local NGO providing affordable housing for the poor. Even though it was mostly commission-based, making the pay somewhat low or inconsistent at times, my colleagues and I still felt content and motivated by the work. The deputy director of the organization, a very kind gentleman in his forties, was welcoming to us and made sure we felt comfortable. On my first arrival, he had introduced me to my colleagues, and I quickly felt like a part of the organization. Realizing that it was my first time in Abidjan, he invited my colleague and me to join him for a tour that weekend.

We met him in the morning and were taken on a boat ride through the middle of Abidjan and then to a church that was holding a beautiful festival. We stopped to watch for a while.

Everyone wore white outfits and danced. It was a four-hour event and featured various speakers and musical performances, a festive and informative way to get to know the culture. We were introduced to his wife and daughter, who were also part of the ceremony, as well as many church members. Everyone was friendly to me and made me feel accepted within their community. The church was spotless, decorated for the festival in attractive colors and details. This serene and unique experience was a cheerful salutation to my first week in Côte d'Ivoire.

After the festival, my guide invited me to his home, where his wife had prepared fried plantain for all of us. Their eight-year-old daughter chattered away beside me, practicing her English. It was a heartwarming evening to find myself in such a loving family atmosphere as a newcomer to this country. When he called me a taxi, he even paid the fare. As I was driven back to my home, I felt truly touched and marveled that someone I had barely known for a week had welcomed me with such open arms into his home.

In the office, he was equally thoughtful and helpful. The next day he took me out to lunch to explain the company policies and operations. But I was worried when, for the next two days, he did not come into the office. When I asked around, I learned that his wife had suddenly passed away.

At first, I thought that I had misunderstood — I was still unfamiliar with the French-Ivorian accent — but when colleagues confirmed the news, I could hardly believe it. Had it not been only four days since she had prepared lunch for us in such a blissful setting?

After a week passed, I sent him a message of condolence. He replied with thanks for the wishes. A colleague and I decided to visit his place and personally extend our condolences. His grief was apparent — he looked frail and talked little, contrasting sharply to his previous personality. His daughter was absolutely silent, not speaking to us at all, and she appeared to still be in shock. After we refused his offer of food, he told us the details of his wife's untimely passing.

A day after the church ceremony, his wife had felt aches in her stomach, but because the pain wasn't severe, he decided to still go into the office. Later that afternoon, she called him to report that she was going to the hospital to get a checkup. The pain was worse and not subsiding. He offered to meet her there.

While he was on the way, his wife called him, saying that the pain was unbearable, and she was not getting any medical attention. He told her to pass the phone to the nearest nurse. The nurse explained that she had appendicitis and needed an urgent operation, but they were not allowed to operate on her unless he paid the fees upfront. He assured her that he was bringing the money with him, and he was nearly there. He begged the nurse to start the surgery. But the medical staff didn't agree to the request, refusing to begin her treatment until he arrived with the money.

She had died by the time he arrived at the hospital.

What seems like such an avoidable and terrible situation is regrettably very common in medical centers in developing and conflict zones. Even in his anger, sorrow, and frustration, he couldn't carry out any legal action against the hospital for this harsh policy. Despite having a decent income, he had to bear the loss of his wife just because he wasn't physically present to pay the hospital. The terrible timing was all it had taken for his wife to needlessly lose her life.

After hearing this story, I felt disgusted at how easily she could have been saved in a different scenario. The repercussions of a healthcare system that prioritizes money over human life are devastating.

When I arrived home and told the story to my host, he nodded in recognition. In Abidjan, during the civil war, a lot of hospital staff had rejected patients for similar reasons. The townspeople suffered from hundreds of casualties that could have been easily avoided. The episode opened my eyes to the imbalanced health industry in these parts of the world and the terrible losses a family can suffer from a profit-driven clinic that doesn't serve the people.

In Afghanistan, too, I felt that the hospitals were always overcrowded with lines of people desperate for medical attention, suffering, and dying while they waited. Those who had funds would travel to India or Pakistan for superior treatments, but the rest would have to suffer because of the country's overextended medical system, pushed to the breaking point by the casualties of war.

Fig. 29 A church ceremony in Abidjan, Côte d'Ivoire

Defense Against Deadly Beasts

I had more than one near-death experience in Ghana. Although, this time, the danger didn't come from fellow humans. Also, this time the danger was right in my own home.

The WHO estimates that about 9,000 people get bitten by snakes each year in Ghana. It has been estimated that one million snake bites occur every year in Africa, resulting in up to 500,000 envenomations and 30,000 deaths. Snake bites are an issue in every household in rural Africa. From what I observed, in Walewale, nearly everyone has a friend or family member who has died from a snake bite; sadly, many of them children. The active and working population is most at risk, especially farmers, but this sneaky and deadly creature can sink its fangs into anyone when you least expect it.

Knowing this risk, I had cleared the area around my house of all tall bushes. I had burned the dry foliage, as advised by neighbors, to ensure no snakes could hide. I made a habit of always checking my shoes before sliding my feet in, always checking the bedsheets, and even checking the pots in the kitchen before cooking.

But one day, I arrived home from work and slid off my shoes as usual. As I padded through the living room, I glanced at something on the floor: a small piece of wrapper from a cookie box. But when I tried to pick it up, it started to move. This was no wrapper at all, but a colorful baby snake. I trembled with adrenaline, stunned. This was my first time actually seeing a snake, and it was incredibly close. I had been told in the past that snakes couldn't see well, so as it wriggled across the room, I froze, motionless. I began to step backward, away from the creature slowly.

At the door, I shouted for my neighbor. Thankfully, he was just outside. A kind, elderly man who still had strength in his build. I kept calling his name in a panic, feeling my skin crawl and itch with nervous sweat. Even though I knew most snakes couldn't hear, they can feel vibrations.

The elderly man came over to me at the door, asking what was wrong. I pointed toward the snake. His lips momentarily pressed together, perhaps with an idea, before he promptly turned around.

African people in rural areas are fearless when dealing with situations like these since it's a threat they've experienced since childhood. The man quickly and matter-of-factly grabbed a large stone right by the front door, then headed confidently over to the snake. Focusing on the creature which had become still, itself likely trying to avoid being seen, he lifted his rock above his head and threw it down with a tremendous force that came crashing down on the snake's head. Now, the head of a snake can still bite even hours after being separated from the body. He picked up the stone and struck again to make sure that the snake was dead. Then he picked it up with his wrinkly, bare hands and tossed the limp thing outside. My eyes went wide at him. The courage of this old man amazed me.

Appreciative, I paid him a few cedis (local Ghanaian currency) for his timely assistance, and to show him my gratitude.

I realized that if I had to stay longer in rural Africa and stay safe while at it, I would need to learn how to deal with such situations. I further researched snakes and found that the more colorful the snake, the more dangerous. Venomous snakes typically have a more triangular head, whereas non-venomous snakes have a rounded jaw. Also, younger snakes can be even more hazardous than adults because they're small and hard to see, and are born without a rattle. Also, baby snakes will inject all of their venoms at once, because they don't know how to ration it.

I soon realized that these animals were not seeking out humans; they only attack if they feel threatened. My new rule of thumb is to avoid them as much as possible and only take the initiative to defend myself if they cannot be avoided.

During the early days in Ghana, I had been warned about scorpions. Scorpions love darkness and moisture. They find their way inside houses through pipe drains and the plumbing system and can be found in the kitchen or the bathroom. They often hide in shoes. I had read that there are at least 6-7 reported deaths in Ghana because of scorpion bites every year, and one of the biggest scorpions in the world, called an "Emperor Scorpion" is actually found in Ghana. They are known for their docile behavior and almost harmless sting, which can be painful but not poisonous. Only about 25 of the 1,500 known scorpions' species can deliver fatal stings, but you must still always seek medical attention.

However, I wasn't thinking about all of these things that day in my shower. My eyes were barely open, and I was enjoying the relaxing sensation of water running down my back when I sensed something near my foot. I looked down, and there it was — a brown scorpion crawling right next to my leg. This was the first time I had encountered a scorpion in my life, and it caught me entirely by surprise. Rather than panic and scream for help, I gathered my strength and quickly smashed it with a bucket. I was becoming more like the locals every day.

Fig. 30 Baby snake on the floor in Walewale, Ghana

Fig. 31 House in Walewale, Ghana

Traveling in Disguise

In Afghanistan, threats to foreigners are common, especially if you are a journalist or someone working for a religious organization, and worse if it's one the Taliban doesn't support. I'd heard of the dangers — foreign visitors kidnapped for ransom, murdered, or even attacked with acid for acting in any way against the Taliban. One has to be very low-profile when involved in projects in this country, even well-meaning ones that support development or equality. To protect me during my visits to rural areas, where I was often traveling to conduct field monitoring, my colleagues gave me a fake Muslim name. This was a precaution in case the Taliban stopped and questioned us. I liked my "new" name, which was Anwar Mohajir. It sounded like my name Ankur Mahajan, and it would be easy to remember.

I took steps to play the part of this new Muslim character. My name went along well with the disguise I took on in public. I always dressed in traditional Afghan clothes – a long, loose-fitting linen top with matching linen pants underneath. I also wore a scarf and had a beard. It was hard for someone outside of my colleagues to recognize that I was not Afghan, but actually Indian. The only weakness in my disguise was my speech, so I tried to stay silent in public.

When I spoke, it was always in Urdu, which made people think I was from Pakistan. Pakistanis are more accepted than other nationalities since there are a lot of them in Afghanistan. This made me feel safer, but I still feared being stopped by the Taliban.

Suppose the Taliban were to stop your car; the first thing they do is speak to you in Pashto. If you don't respond in Pashto or Dari, they demand your name. If you are obviously a foreigner, you are in danger of being kidnapped. But, if your complexion is similar to local Afghans and you have a Muslim name, they may let you go thinking that you're either an Afghan or from Pakistan. Having a Muslim name also makes it easier to call someone in public.

During my work in Afghanistan, all field visits to projects were kept highly confidential. Nobody except your direct supervisor and operations manager had any details. I was not supposed to tell anyone, except the most relevant colleagues, about my specific travel plans, including exact details of arrival and departure. Itineraries are discussed at the last minute by phone through the operations department, to ensure safety. This made requesting travel plans to the next field visit challenging. To start the process, I would let the operations staff know the next location I wished to visit. Then, I would wait with no further information. Finally, I would get a call simply telling me I was to head out the next day.

It became important always to keep my luggage at hand, stocked with passport, at least $300-400 cash, and clothes for three to four days. Also, it is recommended to carry a burqa as a backup in case there is trouble facing the Taliban — a further and more drastic disguise. I always had all of these essentials ready. The day after receiving the phone call notice, I would await a call from the operations department to say that the SUV would arrive for me in 5-10 minutes. All field trips are made by SUVs as the road conditions in rural Afghanistan, and African nations are still some of the worst in the world.

Once the travel begins, security staff would actively determine our route based on intelligence reports. Say a trip from your station was supposed to take five hours of driving. If there were reports of the Taliban in that area, they change the routes, meaning the detour trip might take up to two days. Taliban often set up roadblocks in order to kidnap foreigners or high-profile Afghans. If it wasn't a roadblock, it was a landmine set by the Taliban along a route and obviously a deadly encounter to drive over. No Muslim name or burqa could protect you from a landmine. So, the security staff listened to the reports and often changed routes. All of these intelligence reports came from Kabul continuously, where all international organizations had their own security and intelligence networks.

Each journey, I would grip my bag with white knuckles, on alert for any instruction and praying for safe passage. Despite all of the precautions that we had taken, the danger was real and common for many foreigners in Afghanistan at the time. Each journey felt like a gamble, and each successful arrival felt like I'd narrowly slipped through a deadly trap.

Hotel Park Palace Incident on 13th May 2015

My work in international development has included visits to some of the most dangerous places in the world. From Sub-Saharan Africa to Afghanistan, I experienced and witnessed the daily hardships of many people in these regions. From terrorism and corruption to the lack of basic medical care, people struggle to survive in these areas. Death and loss are far more present.

In May 2015, I came to Kabul to attend a conference via a domestic flight from Fayzabad, Badakhshan. It was the summer — the Taliban was particularly active during those months of heat. Almost every day, they took lives. Attacks targeted markets, shopping areas, and hospitals, along with government buildings. No place was safe, and people lived in constant fear under the threat of death. The instability of the country affected the everyday lives and needs of all living in these conflict zones.

I had stayed at the popular Hotel Park Palace in central Kabul before, and I was always happy to come to Kabul from Fayzabad. Kabul offered a great selection of diverse cuisine that I looked forward to enjoying, even though during this time of threat, expatriates were not allowed to dine in restaurants, and all food was delivered to your home or hotel. Kabul had a much better social life than the smaller town of Fayzabad, so I also anticipated my exploration of the historic city of bazaars, mosques, gardens, and palaces, as I find them intriguing and engaging.

Since I had stayed in that hotel many times before, I knew my way around it, and I knew the staff and felt comfortable accordingly. My room was adequate, and the buffet food was decent, but the customer service had fallen off since my last stay. I considered the option of finding an alternative lodging for any future visits here.

After first arriving, exhausted from travel, I slept for a few hours before attending a work conference. The conference centered on the progress of development grants and included donors in the event and conversations. Then, during dinner back at the hotel, I chatted with several other guests.

There was a young lady from Kazakhstan with an Italian friend, along with a few Indians and some Pakistanis. We filled our plates from the dinner buffet and discussed our backgrounds and the culture of Afghanistan. We discussed some developmental issues at hand in the country and compared them to others — most professionals traveling in Kabul have experiences in other developing countries to share. I also chatted with some friendlier hotel staff members, though in these conversations, I was always careful to limit my personal opinions when talking about development and diplomacy.

Through my travels, I have developed a keen sense of intuition when it comes to trusting others. Not all of my thoughts needed or should have been shared aloud, depending on the company.

After dinner, I returned to my room to pack for the next trip. After a light breakfast the next day, I left for the airport to catch the UN flight back to Fayzabad. Upon arriving at the airport, I learned that the flight had been canceled. I was frustrated but not too shocked, as

UN flight cancelations are relatively common, especially if there are security risks or inclement weather potential. Because the passengers on these UN domestic flights are usually workers representing non-governmental or international organizations, even the slight possibility of a terrorist attack will ground a flight.

Disappointed about the cancellation, I returned to the Hotel Park Palace and tried to relax, hoping that I would fly out of Kabul the following day. The next day followed almost the same pattern, although I made it a bit further at the airport. After clearing airport security and waiting to board, the flight was again canceled. I returned to a long check-in queue at the hotel, but because I knew the staff and routine well, I dropped my ID with the clerk and asked for the application to be filled out. I took my room key and planned to return later to pick up my ID.

At dinner, I was again able to chat with my acquaintances from Kazakhstan, Pakistan, and India. The young lady from Kazakhstan and the Italian gentleman were visiting Afghanistan for the filming of a documentary. I spoke to them for half an hour or so, making friendly and interesting conversation while we dined. The conversation often flows with ease with other international workers in these conflict zones, as there is so much to relate to as fellow foreigners in a unique country.

As we talked, it came up that there would be a concert the following night featuring a famous Afghan classical musician. I half hoped that the flight would be canceled again so I could attend. The next morning we tried the same routine again — a colleague, and I departed for the Kabul airport. After passing through the initial security stages with my ticket and passport, I then had to present my organizational ID to fully complete the UN boarding requirements. I frantically searched my wallet and bag for the ID and, in a panic, realized that I had never returned to pick it up from the hotel clerk.

The flight was departing in less than an hour, and I didn't have enough time to make it to the hotel and back.

Missing this flight would mean that I would not be able to return to Fayzabad for at least a couple more days. With the flight already canceled twice before, it was lucky to be taking off this particular day at all. I was feeling hopeless at the security gate when my colleague suggested calling the company driver and asking if he could deliver the ID to the airport for me. I sat in the airport staring at the clock with stress, doubtful he would make it in time. But a wave of relief washed over me as I saw the driver pull up with ID in hand, just in time for the flight. I was finally out of Kabul on my way back to Fayzabad.

Upon arrival, I returned straight to the office to catch up on work, which had fallen behind from the unexpected delays in Kabul. By now, I had already spent two years working in the Fayzabad office. It felt good to be back in my familiar station after traveling for a few days. I had been focused on my work for some time when a colleague stepped in to inform me that the Taliban had just attacked the Hotel Park Palace in Kabul.

Shocked, I dropped everything and instantly flipped on the television to a live news report. I shivered as I heard that several gunmen had entered the premises right before the concert. I was filled with a kind of terrified gratitude as I thought about the last-minute delivery of my ID to the airport, and how narrowly I'd caught my flight out. I had been so close to spending another night at that hotel in Kabul. I would have been at that concert.

My colleague and I were fixated on the television reports for the next several hours, even after almost everyone had left the office. According to a statement by the Taliban, "the attack was planned carefully to target the concert party in which important foreign dignitaries were attending." They killed auditors hired by the Afghan government and many others. The gunmen went from room to room, searching for foreigners during the attack, which lasted over six hours.

Fourteen people were killed in the attack, including the young lady from Kazakhstan, the Italian gentleman, and the Indians and Pakistanis whom I had just spoken with only a short time ago.

We had connected in Kabul so casually, like friends, knowing nothing of the coming attack. We had shared laughs and conversed about our lives and experiences. Now, I felt an emptiness thinking about them, floored by the loss of those lives in Kabul just a few hours before. I had narrowly been spared. This terrifying event made me realize the fragility and uncertainty of life, that one moment you can be happily chatting with new friends and just a short time later find yourself in an unexpected and life-taking attack. It personally impressed on me the idea that each day should not be taken for granted. It can all end at any moment. It had ended for some on the 13th of May in 2015. But I would return to my bed safely that night.

Fig. 32 13th May 2015—Fayzabad airport, returning after several cancellations on the day of the attack on Park Palace, via UN helicopter

Stampede in Abidjan Market and Ouagadougou

Another international adventure had brought me to the western African country of Côte d'Ivoire. The country is diverse and includes the major ethnic groups of the Akan and the Mande. The former French colony is also home to followers of Islam, Christianity, and traditional African religions. Although initially shocked by the culture of Côte d'Ivoire, friendly locals helped me to understand the customs and culture, and I eventually adapted and became more comfortable.

The country seemed like it was still in recovery from recent conflict. Côte d'Ivoire erupted in a civil war in 2002, and tensions finally settled in 2009. During my time in the country, there was a powerful military and police presence and a general atmosphere of fear. I think that I felt just as vulnerable as any other person living in the country.

The city of Abidjan is the economic center of Côte d'Ivoire and has a vivacious market. A visit to the market with a few friends from the University of Cocody exposed me to the vibrancy of exchange among the buyers and sellers. The place was filled with the shouting of prices and the rustle of transport, people hurrying by to get the best products. Women were selling fresh fish, chicken, and all bushmeat varieties from the side of the street. The intense smell of the marketplace overwhelmed me.

I stood out like a sore thumb — an obvious foreigner. This attracted a lot of attention my way. Locals questioned me about the fashion of my clothing and shoes. I was even offered marriage proposals as several suggested their daughters as prospective wives for myself. The friendliness of the locals and the market environment made for an enjoyable walk with my university friends.

However, as we continued through the market, taking in the sights and sounds, a loud shout suddenly rang above the normal noise. People's faces turned fearful, and the area descended into chaos. Confusion took over, I couldn't make sense of what was happening. There was panic in the crowd, words were garbled, people were breathlessly running, and some had begun to speak in their tribal languages out of fear.

A wall of people ran at full speed toward us, which started a chain reaction as others joined in. My heart raced — there was little room to move in the confined market space, and even the local police officials had begun to run. So, my friends and I turned and ran as well. Amid the confusion, one of my friends suggested that we take cover under a bus. I was in shock at this point and willingly followed his direction. After a half-hour undercover, the situation had calmed down, so we emerged from the bus. The experience of uncertainty shook me in such an uncontrollable situation. We hailed the first available taxi and left immediately.

We later learned that the stampede had claimed the lives of twelve people. The cause was not determined, but my friends informed me that market stampedes are relatively common and often take the lives of the elderly and children who can't easily get out of the way. The people here are continually fearful of resumed military actions. When suspecting a riot, armed soldiers often fire into enormous crowds, and they sometimes kill innocent people while the military is not held responsible for these deaths. People are ever fearful of sudden attacks by the army or rebels, and there's a short fuse to panic. There is little sense of security in these conflicted environments, even as one goes about their daily activities at the market. Unfortunately, these incidents are widespread but rarely get reported in the media.

A visit to Ouagadougou in Burkina Faso further impressed upon me the significant instability in some developing countries. While visiting there, a gathering of people was protesting the dictatorial rule of President Blaise Compaoré. The president routinely repressed any dissent to his power with drastic or violent actions. Opposition to his policies resulted in jailing, torture, and murder. This particular protest was located in the middle of a roundabout near a noteworthy city monument.

I was only visiting for a short time, and my curiosity led me closer to see what was happening. Protesters held banners with slogans that opposed the rule of Compaoré. The young protesters, most in their twenties or thirties and likely university students, were loud and boisterous. I observed them chanting, marching, and giving speeches for about fifteen minutes when gunshots suddenly rang out. Protestors dispersed in panic, and I realized that government soldiers had opened fire on the crowd.

Fear struck everyone. I ran, even though I wasn't involved in the demonstration. Remembering my experience in the Abidjan market, I realized that I had to separate myself from the crowd to survive. As I ran, I spotted a local theater and hid behind the building until the situation settled.

I saw people scrambling for safety. Some were attempting to climb walls, trees, and lamp poles. The scene around me felt too sudden and dramatic to be real, like I was watching a film or documentary. But it was real; I was right at the center of the chaos. The gunshots lasted for five minutes, but I hid behind the theater for over an hour. When I finally emerged, the situation had calmed. Unbelievably, regular activity had resumed as if nothing had happened. It was as if the whole affair was just a temporary distraction from the usual daily activity. I was stunned and unsure of what to think. Ultimately, I realized that this was the norm, and the people in this area had simply accustomed themselves to it. Shops had reopened, lives continued, and everyone was going about their daily affairs.

As I walked through the city, I could hear ambulances. Perhaps medics were rescuing or tending to the wounded? There were hundreds of posters plastered all over walls in the city that protested the government. The signs expressed grievances in French: the official language of the country. I continued my walk through the city, now placid and undisturbed, but a new level of alertness had seeded itself in my mind.

Later that evening, I learned from the local television report that five people had been killed during the protest. The information did not include the causes of the deaths, but I felt that it was the same to assume that the deceased had been struck by the bullets. As I was watching the news, I recalled the crack of gunshots and involuntarily winced. The media didn't disclose the number of injured people earlier that day, and I suspected that the casualties were likely higher. The government probably apprehended some protestors, but none of this was reported.

This was my first experience with government suppression of the media. Governments in developing countries often hide these kinds of events from the outside world. Leaders fear the loss of reputation and, ultimately, power. After what I experienced that day in Ouagadougou, I realized the wisdom of staying away from such protests and events. Situations can unravel quickly, and even though I had not been involved, too much curiosity can be life-threatening. Conflicted countries often lack the rule of law and a fair individual system, and the media is under immense pressure from the government. It is not a place where you want to get caught up in an arrest, or worse, trampled or shot in a panicked crowd.

Although there is so much instability, corruption, and danger in conflicted countries, I have found that people are unusually resilient. The locals who make up these areas continue to live their daily lives amid surrounding violence. They cannot succumb to constant fear, or their lives would effectively become paralyzed. From my observations, I have noticed that people in these areas appreciate the small things in life. They are survivors and heroically manage to make the best out of nearly impossible circumstances.

Fig. 33 Protest at UN Globe roundabout in Ouagadougou, Burkina Faso minutes before the shooting

All Badakhshan 5km Run

Truly one of the most memorable experiences of my life was organizing the first All Badakhshan 5km Run Challenge in Afghanistan. Being an advocate for physical activity, I always wanted to promote healthy living through regular exercise and diet. I was looking for great ways to promote this lifestyle, celebrate fitness, and unite people through physical movement. So, I decided to organize a race in the capital city of Fayzabad with 50 athletes in 2015. My organization received a development grant from the USAID, United States Agency for International Development, with which this long-time dream could finally be realized.

Establishing the Run Challenge was complicated: there was detailed planning regarding route selection, athlete qualification, prize selection, media coverage, logistics, and security. While there were initial confusion and challenges, we overcame them through a coordinated team effort. I made sure that every individual in the organizing committee was delegated a significant responsibility, and I also conducted periodic meetings with everyone to ensure ongoing progress. A week before the event, dignitaries were invited to attend. The invitees included government figures, Mullahs (religious leaders), NGO heads, Olympic committee members, and Civil Society association representatives. In order to ensure the success of this event, I made sure that all the important people of the province were invited.

The event was initially planned to be held on a certain date, but just two days before then, we decided to have it a day earlier. This may seem like a strange last-minute change, but this was a strategy to mitigate security concerns. The Taliban notoriously disrupted public events such as this, and we were aware of the danger they posed. Secondly, we wanted to hold the event on Friday — it is a weekly holiday in Afghanistan. We organizers felt that holding the event on holiday would attract more spectators and be more traffic-friendly.

The route was mapped out to ensure the distance was precisely five kilometers. I personally had wanted a half-marathon event, but again due to the fear of Taliban disruption, we planned to allow the event to end early and avoid further risk for an attack. The banner for the competition was put up at 7:30 AM, and athletes were asked to line up by 8:00 AM. Spectators enjoyed comfortable seating, and energy vibrated through the crowd as background music pumped up the athletes and onlookers. All preparations were complete.

Soon the invitees, technical committee, and athletes gathered at the center of the city. It was enthralling, as I had never organized an event of this magnitude previously. The colorful crowd of happy attendees, the arrival of local leaders and heroes, and the excited athletes lining up were all incredibly inspiring to me. I'd helped to create an experience for everyone in the community to enjoy.

Soon after, the participating athletes, camera operators, photographers, and technical staff were transported to the starting line on rented buses, cars, and motorbikes. I had around one hundred Afghan National Force soldiers and police cars deployed to enforce road closures and ensure athletes' safety. But despite the careful planning and the jovial atmosphere, I was still anxious about a potential attack. If there were any casualties, I would have felt guilty for the rest of my life. Remembering all of the sudden and tragic twists I'd experienced throughout my global living, I couldn't help but think about how quickly this bright scene could turn to horror.

Nevertheless, I had planned as well as I could have for any scenario. I surveyed the scene. Military soldiers were guarding all the streets blocked off for the course, but I knew it was common for Taliban suicide bombers to disguise themselves. My other heavy concern was if an insider from our team was a Taliban spy and had given them information in advance to facilitate an attack.

The race event took three hours from start to completion. Those three hours were probably the most stressful of my life. While everyone watched, cheered, and celebrated, my eyes scanned the area for signs of danger, and my ears listened for screams or gunshots.

The local hospital also provided us with a medical ambulance, in case of an athlete injury. Of course, the ambulance was also there in case there was a Taliban attack. All of the athletes were given green shirts to identify them as racers. I was in the back of a jeep that was leading them to the course. I remember cheers from people all around Fayzabad who had come out in the streets to support their local athletes. This was incredible to see. People of Afghanistan love sporting events, but ongoing security concerns result in very few of these events being held in their country.

The race was planned to end in the middle of the city center. The loudspeaker on my car was leading them, and we were providing running commentary along with continuous motivational slogans. The cheers of the crowd grew louder as the end of the 5 km course approached us.

When the leading athlete managed to win by a significant margin, his finish was met with victorious roars from the crowd. All contestants finished the race within 45 minutes. When they all had crossed the finish line, I felt an enormous weight lift off of my shoulders: there had been no injuries, no attacks, no problems. It was as if air had re-entered my lungs after hours of holding my breath. Now I could enjoy myself and revel in this rewarding experience, glowing from the fact that I — with others — successfully made this happen for everyone. I clapped along with spectators, cheered with my fellow colleagues, and cherished this experience of collective celebration.

There was still the ceremony left, which meant a new round of anxiety on my part. I watched as everybody came together and formed a circle around the stage where prizes were to be presented. The ceremony lasted for only half an hour, but I was praying every minute of it, for it to pass smoothly without any deadly interruptions. After the winners were awarded their prizes, all participants received a certificate of participation, presented to them by organizers and dignitaries. Speeches on the importance of leading a healthy lifestyle followed the award ceremony. Medals were given to key organizers by the Olympic Committee — including myself. I looked upon the many satisfied faces of attendees, and I felt proud for what we had all accomplished. My medal from the Olympic Committee remains a prized possession, and one of my greatest achievements, mainly due to the fact that it was awarded for community development. I felt absolutely ecstatic.

The event concluded in a brief interview with the Afghan National Channel. This was my opportunity to explain how the event was organized and emphasize the importance of good health in everyone's life. I emphasized that we should encourage young people to take part in sports. It would be an essential part of establishing peace in the country.

The event was praised by everyone, including local residents of the Civil Society Association, Olympic Committee, and other dignitaries. Athletes and spectators all rejoiced in the opportunity to forget their troubles and celebrate human fitness for a day. The event was a brilliant campaign for further promoting public sports and provided a powerful argument for building better sports facilities. I also believe that the sporting event fostered the spirit of competition and friendship between peoples.

Yes, there were security constraints in the country, limited resources for athletes, and a weak national government. But I believe there still exists a tremendous amount of talent and potential amongst our youth. People are still people, with passions and talents and dreams like anyone else. This race attracted the best Badakhshan athletes who battled it out to claim the honor of being the fastest 5km runner in the province. It was the first time that an official running event was conducted on the streets of Fayzabad on a larger scale. Most importantly, the success of the event persuaded the Olympic committee to establish a running federation in Badakhshan.

I later realized that the event had only males. All the audiences, athletes, and dignitaries were men. There were hardly any female viewers. Any woman I saw that day was simply coming or going to the local markets and had just paused for a few minutes to look at the event. I remember seeing a little girl, eyes glimmering with intrigue, looking down at the event from a high window in her house. She was almost bouncing as the runners began to approach her street, and she could surely hear the booming claps and shouts of the onlookers down below. Then she noticed that I'd spotted her — I waved with a friendly smile, then she immediately closed the curtains. My heart sunk, seeing that flash of fear in her eyes before the curtains drawn. It felt painful that she had mistakenly felt that I didn't want her to see the race. While the event had gone really well, I was struck that girls and women had a considerably hard life here and weren't even allowed to attend recreational public events.

Looking back at the event, I felt one of the key reasons for its success and safety was that it was done with the collaboration of other civil societies and religious leaders. Therefore, it looked like an Afghan initiative and had nothing to do with other countries. This is very important; when another country is involved in an event, it can be perceived as an initiative by outsiders to influence the Afghan people and undermine their culture. Despite resistance from many who warned me that this could be fatal, I was grateful that I went with the idea to do this for the community. The race will forever be an achievement I cherish and a reminder that I shouldn't take for granted my many opportunities to pursue the activities I love. My heart will always ache for those living in parts of the world where it is far more challenging to follow a dream.

Fig. 34 1st All Badakhshan 5 KM Run Challenge

Fig. 35 Athletes Line up at 5km All Badakhshan Run Challenge

Fig. 36 *Afghan National Force soldiers and police cars deployed to enforce road closures and escort athletes, while thousands of male spectators enjoy the event.*

Fig. 37 *Receiving organizers medal from Afghan Olympic committee on the national TV in 2015 for organizing 1st All Badakhshan 5KM race*

The Late-Night Caller

Throughout my time in Afghanistan and sub-Saharan Africa, life-threatening encounters were not uncommon. While each one was shocking, they provided new insight and a unique lesson that has left me stronger to this day.

In 2009, I was visiting a small village near Dabou, Yamoussoukro, in Côte d'Ivoire. The town and people were abuzz with excitement — the Nouveau Generation festival was to take place. I'd been invited by a friend, and we had taken the bus from Abidjan, where I was stationed for work.

Immediately off the bus, the welcome was warm, and the atmosphere was full of celebration. As the only foreigner, I got a lot of special attention and kind treatment. People grabbed my hands and greeted me with bright eyes. The festival lasted several days, filled with unique cultural dances, celebrations, décor, and music. That happy feeling of living in the here and now, enjoying the day, and feeling warmth towards friends and strangers around you was contagious. None of us seemed to be worried about the future, at least during this festival. Making friends, dancing, and eating well, I came to decide that Ivorians are very joyous and fun-loving folk.

Eventually, all the celebrations left me exhausted. On the last night, I headed back to my room with tender feet and a heavy body, happy but wanting sleep. Just as I was pulling myself into bed, the echo of the festival music still lingering in my head, I heard a knock on the door.

It was a girl about 17 years old. She was well-dressed in a skirt with leggings and a blacktop. It startled me as it was late, and I wasn't expecting anyone, let alone this stranger. She greeted me in French, then helped herself inside.

I racked my brain as to why she might be here — *had I met her at the festival? Had I made a plan that I forgot? Did she have a message for me?*

Many villagers in Côte d'Ivoire speak only their local dialect and like to practice their English when they meet foreigners. *Was she here to practice her English? But why now, so late?*

My foggy, over-stimulated brain was slow to understand the situation. In my confusion, I closed the door and sat back down on the bed. She immediately sat down beside me. Realizing the awkward silence, I pointed at a magazine featuring American President Obama's picture on the cover. I asked the girl if she knew about him. She insisted that she and everyone in the village liked him. Then I asked her what she did, and she responded that she takes care of a shop owned by her father in the village.

At that point, she moved closer to me and placed her hand on mine. I finally realized that she wasn't there to practice her English language skills. She smiled up at me as her hand left mine and went to the buttons on her top. She began slipping the buttons open and undressing. I immediately told her to stop. This came as a surprise to her; she looked confused. I asked her why she had come here, and she responded that other people in the village sent her to sleep with me.

I was flabbergasted and must have looked as if she'd just punched me in the face. The girl stood half-dressed, looking confused, and unsure about what to do. Just a few days back, I had delivered a lecture on Gender Equality at the University of Cocody. And now here I was, alone in my room with a minor. This felt all wrong, and I wondered if I had actually made it to sleep, and this was some bizarre dream.

But the girl stood there, looking increasingly distressed with her mouth pulled down into a pout. Her body language became less confident, and she crossed her arms over her stomach. I politely told her that it was late, I was tired, and she should leave. This only made her more upset. She stepped away from me with her hands over her face. I continued on, making excuses so she wouldn't think I was rejecting her. I had to get up early; I was so tired, and so on. She finally picked up her purse and left, and as she stepped out the door, it darkened her face with hurt.

The truth was, I really had plans in the morning, and when I awoke, I headed out for breakfast planned in my honor. I began talking with a colleague at my table, beginning with cheery memories of the festivities. But weighing heavy on my mind, I eventually brought up the episode of my late-night caller. As I finished the story, my African colleagues laughed. She was what is called a cadeau (French for "gift") for me, they explained. It was a local tradition to send a young girl to share the night with an honored male guest in the village, to make him happy. It's considered an act of hospitality, and a common "gift" bestowed by doting hosts.

Upon further research, I found that this tradition of Cadeau actually started during the colonial times. French, English, and other European men were considered "masters" and would sleep with younger minor women, thus abusing their power as slave owners. Soon this became a ritual, and many people in the village learned to accept the concept that all foreign men would be pleased to sleep with a local young girl. Unfortunately, colonialism resulted not just in economic damage for the country but a feeling of inferiority amongst the African population. Colonialism had also created an atmosphere where sex is used as a weapon by the slave owners to create hierarchy and class division against the oppressed.

While the breakfast continued and the rest of the table laughed the story away, I couldn't help but feel the immense cultural repercussions of colonialism. It was painful to know that such abuses in history have passed through to the modern-day. While the festival had allowed me to partake in some beautiful and happy traditions of this culture, my late-night visitor had opened my eyes to the darker ones.

Fig. 38 Nouveau Generation Festival celebration in the village of Yamoussoukro, Côte d'Ivoire

Ghanaian Witch Camps

Another unique experience in Ghana took place in Gambaga, a small town in the East Mamprusi District. This is where I visited one of the witch camps. These are residential camps for women accused of witchcraft who have been disowned by their families.

Ghana is one of the top ten most religious countries in the world, and with religion comes superstition. Regrettably, it is not uncommon for Ghanaian people to see misfortune as a result of black magic. Many common life occurrences — death, disease, alcoholism, mental illness (a poorly understood issue), a poor crop yield, or loss of livestock — can result in suspicions of witchcraft. I noticed that if somebody fell ill, the first thing many would often do was to accuse someone they disliked of using dark magic, or juju, to cause their bad luck. The women blamed for witchcraft are typically older or are widows who no longer benefited from the protection of men, or those from polygamous homes who shared a husband with other women. Unfortunately, these individuals are easy targets for false accusations, and many end up exiled in the camps.

In these witch camps, the small community of women are often physically exploited and work for free. Work commands are given to them by the Chief of the village or senior "witch." Many of these accused women have lived in the camps for over 40 years, with some even bringing their children to live with them there. Their miserable lives are very repetitive, doing activities like cooking, cleaning, and other chores for meager or no amount of money, and with no potential for rising out of their situation.

Any woman accused and convicted of black magic can end up in the witch camp. It is a constant threat for the women of Ghana. Also, because polygamy is a common practice in this country, men sometimes take on more wives than they can take care of. Often when a man grows tired of an older wife, he accuses her of witchcraft and easily disposes of her to the camps. Alternatively, if the wives don't get along, jealousy or rivalry can cause them to accuse each other of witchcraft. The women with little support from their husbands or other male relatives find themselves very vulnerable during these attacks, with little power to protect themselves against exile.

Although the Ghanaian government has been trying to shut down these witch camps all around the country, the superstitious culture and rampant sexism allow them to thrive. Such camps provide somewhere to house the so-called "witches," who would otherwise have no options. So, the real question and struggle remain: *What needs to happen to stop people from accusing women of witchcraft?*

It seems that people have to be educated about this particular matter so that they can distinguish between fact and fantasy. Kids need to be taught in school that witchcraft is a falsehood and a superstition and to see such accusations as nonsense. Educated leaders in the villages could stand up for accused women and call out the falsehood of these claims.

Once the new generations of Ghanaian citizens understand that these concepts are fictitious, the accusations should decrease, and the need for witch camps should then, hopefully, disappear.

March for Gender Equality

While my experience with the medical profession was rough, I had an equally memorable experience that makes me proud of how I was able to contribute to those in need. There was a March for Gender Equality being held in Walewale, Ghana, an event that I helped to organize. I encountered many very ambitious women during my stay in Walewale, but there weren't many women in positions of power. The apparent disparity of gender roles made some start to consider what was needed to help promote women to positions of leadership, and the solution many of us felt would raise awareness was an organized march.

Ghanaian history is full of women who have played essential roles, from armed conflicts to nurses, and every position between combatants and workers. It is impossible to overstate women's contributions, particularly during times of peace. Far too often, their efforts have gone unrecognized and remain undervalued, primarily because they take place outside official or high-level forums. Nor are the activities that they typically undertake traditionally associated with peace-building.

As a result, women's skills, insights, and energy are too often overlooked, not just in Ghana but across the world. However, we were focused on building up the women in Ghana because they had a long history of improving the nation. The result of hiding women's accomplishments is a misleading image that women are merely victims of conflict and that they are simply passive beneficiaries of interventions. We felt that this false belief should be actively changed to highlight the actual role of women in establishing peace and stability.

Joined by the Peace Corps in the village where I was stationed, as well as some of the nearby villages, we decided to organize the march. International Women's Day was to occur soon after we made this decision, making it easy to establish that as the day that would be the best to raise awareness and bring more attention to the event. The march had the support of Langum Women Association, a local association of women largely composed of single-parent widows trying their best to build their lives and bring stability to the lives of their children after losing their husbands.

This event had no security threat: Ghana is typically a peaceful nation. The march commenced at 8:00 AM on 7th July 2013 at the Walewale Hospital, with the full march route including a distance of 5 km. The march involved more than 100 people from the community, including school children and government officials. I rode on a bike in front of the march, where I ended up being incredibly impressed by the response. It was fascinating to see all the people wearing slogans of gender equality as they marched along the route — and sometimes the march melded with dancing, making it one of the most unique, memorable, and happy memories of my time in Ghana.

We had been right about how much attention the march would attract. The local band had even volunteered to play while the participants sang, clapped, danced, and chanted slogans to promote our cause. The march participants themselves brought many messages to the event regarding women and girls' empowerment.

The march proved to be the ideal opportunity to underscore the need for political commitment to accelerate action to achieve gender equality. The march ended at about 10 AM at the District Assembly. Upon the march's conclusion, the District Governor of Walewale delivered a speech addressing the importance of having women leaders and their contributions to peace processes — both of which need more significant financial and political support.

The other members of the Assembly gave their speeches emphasizing how crucial it was to provide women and girls with equal access to education, health care, work opportunities, and representation in political and economic decision-making processes. This equality, they reasoned, would benefit Ghanaian society and humanity at large.

The entire march was recorded by the local TV channel and was broadcast live by local radio stations. The success of it thrilled me. One of the greatest outcomes was that it brought the organizers closer together, increasing the likelihood that they would continue to work towards gender equality long after the march had ended.

The success from even humble acts of leadership or kindness can give one greater satisfaction than owning material wealth. I felt proud that this march had inspired and empowered others to work towards social change. The fact that the people there had been so eager and open to the idea was ultimately what made the event so successful. It also showed me how much can be done in rural villages because they really care about the members of their community. They want to provide the best opportunities for everyone to succeed, something that gives me hopes that they will be able to start solving some of the larger systemic issues common to developing nations.

Witness to a Kidnapping

In Ghana, during an election, the tension is thicker than the heat. This being my first time, locals advised me to stock up on two weeks' of food and hide out in my home.

The militia began to appear on the streets, especially in areas of the political divide. Their jeeps roared down the quiet streets while soldiers eyed you as you said hello to a passing neighbor, or stepped outside to hang the laundry, or merely opened a window. But somehow, their presence didn't feel protective, and I soon learned why.

One night I ran out of water and had no choice but to head to the village shop, about 10 minutes away by motorbike. It was early in the evening, and most of the streets in Walewale were empty, except those military jeeps parading army personnel armed with assault rifles.

I finally left my home after four days. It felt like a Hollywood war movie, dark and silent except for the rumbling of jeeps and the chattering of soldiers. My bike's headlight was the only light on my journey to the shop, cutting the darkness just ahead of me. But it was the same as any other trip, so far, and soon I was returning to the motorbike with water bottles in hand.

A girl, probably around sixteen-years-old, was walking on the opposite side of the road as I left the shop. I could see her lit up by a faraway streetlight, though she probably couldn't see me. She was carrying a woven basket on her head, as would many of the African women and young girls in my village. These would hold fish to sell or bread. I assumed she was coming back from the market. During elections, markets closed earlier.

I had just finished tying all the bottles on the rack of my bike and was about to start it up when a military jeep, loaded with seven heavily armed soldiers, pulled up and stopped beside the girl. They drunkenly gestured with their hands and shouted. Their jeep blocked her way, and then three intimidating men shuffled out to corner her. At first, they were just talking, so I considered heading out. But the girl began to flail and scream as the men grabbed her arm. Her basket fell to the street, contents spilling out. A young boy who happened to be walking nearby came over and said something to the soldiers, brow furrowed with anger.

Two of the soldiers were on him right away, kicking his ribs and head while he tried shielding himself with his arms and scrunching up into a ball. Horrified yet helpless, I saw the boy now lying bloodied on the street.

I was about 100 meters from them and under a shade, so they were unable to see me. The soldiers were pushing the girl into the jeep — she was being kidnapped. I stood frozen, half on my motorbike, desperate to step out and help her. Then I looked again at their guns.

As a foreigner, and with no weapon or super strength of my own, I would be squashed as quickly as that boy who lay there groaning on the road. But the girl had no hope except for me.

My indecision turned to shame as the jeep quickly pulled away, the girl still wailing and struggling against the strength of those seven monstrous men. Now I knew why I'd been advised to stay home — these soldiers were not protectors in a time of unrest. They did not bring calm during the elections.

They were the danger.

I hurried to the local Police station, thinking that they could do something about the situation and help both the kidnapped girl and injured boy, but my hopes were dashed at once: it was closed.

I stayed up all night replaying this abduction in my head. The girl was surely going to be raped, and who knows what else would come after that. I prayed that the boy wasn't hurt too severely and that help would find him sooner than later. The next day, I reported the incident to my colleagues and work. Yet the local Ghanaians brushed off the incident, as they know military abuse is rarely disciplined. I couldn't do much and felt crushed because of this. I had no photographs or identification of the men. But I had seen it, could never unsee it, and could only imagine the terror and pain of that poor girl.

For days the episode haunted me. I hated myself for my failure to act, for my overwhelming fear. I still feel the guilt to this day. My Ghanaian colleagues continued to reassure me that I couldn't have done anything about it, that they would have done the same as I had. Everyone knew the men could have killed me and probably would have without even a hint of remorse. Even police never acted against the stationed soldiers, and sexual assaults were commonly unreported and almost always went unpunished.

Ghana, and Africa itself, have been sieged by many military coups in the recent past. People have come to understand the intimidation and violence of the military, and their only defense is to keep their heads down and stay out of the way. Of course, not all of them are like that — the beaten boy, for example — but that episode left a deep impression on me. I had suffered similar encounters with the Ivorian military. To this day, I'm troubled by how much crime power-drunk soldiers will get away with in these developing and conflict areas. And how many women have suffered a fate like a girl I saw on that dark night.

Hospitality Around the World

While many encounters on my travels were full of danger and fear, just as many were filled with beautiful moments of human kindness and hospitality, some people can leave a lasting impression on you with a single act of kindness. People of all races, tribes, and nationalities have been extremely generous to me. While the outer shell of human beings can seem hard, I have found that once you become closer to people; you discover a hidden layer. You realize that your perception of them is often wrong, and they gift you with valuable memories to treasure.

Canada is known as a culture that smiles and waves at strangers. But that doesn't mean everyone takes an instant liking towards you. The old saying about North Americans can be very true: People tend to be friendly, but they are not your friends. People can be slow to get to know you and earn trust. In contrast, many Eastern cultures, especially ex-Soviet countries, tend to not speak or smile at random strangers. This can be a shock to visitors from North America, but that doesn't mean people are rude or disapprove of you; it's just not a part of their culture.

Foreigners will find that it's much easier to make close friendships in the Eastern or African cultures as compared to Western society, mainly because people are more curious to know about your background. They have been brought up in a way to be more social and comfortable speaking to strangers. This is very true in the context of African countries. During my time in Ghana and Côte d'Ivoire, just after a week, I found many people happy to speak to me or help me out. Even when I visited other villages, people would still shake my hand or sometimes hug me, especially little kids, as if I had known them for a very long time.

I encountered no xenophobia towards foreigners in all of the African countries that I lived in or visited. Comparatively, Europe and North America tend to be very reserved towards people of different races or backgrounds, at least initially. I feel one reason for this is that the media in these places is directed more towards finding cautious red flags or in stating the stereotypes than actually just considering everyone as people irrespective of their different races or backgrounds.

In the case of African countries, ignorance can be bliss, allowing people to not see the evil in everyone, but to see them as a fellow human. People who travel and have been exposed to different backgrounds tend to see everyone as individuals and resist stereotypes about the behavior of people from certain countries.

A shining moment of human connection happened to me in 2009, during my initial days in Tashkent, Uzbekistan. I had just arrived in the country and was living in a hotel for the first few days. The plan was to move into an apartment as soon as possible, as the hotel was much too expensive. A friendly staff member of the hotel showed me the city and answered questions about its culture. He merrily explained all the minor aspects of the city, showing me around and taking the time to help me settle in.

Overall, he was warm and had a genuine smile, treating me as an honored guest. He pointed out his favorite shops, popular parks, and meeting points and shared with me the best dishes to try while here. These tips may have taken weeks to find out in other countries, but he happily and willingly shared his knowledge, making me feel welcome instantly. We became good friends in just three days of knowing each other. It only took two days to find an apartment that suited me, thanks to his generous tours and answers.

But unfortunately, as I was packing up back at the hotel, the landlord of the new apartment called to alert me of a paperwork problem. At that time in Tashkent, all foreigners needed to fill out a residence registration with the local police. This registration stamp would go on the passport. Tashkent had very strict rules, and police regularly checked the documents of foreigners, often in the busy parts of the city. Sometimes, like the Tajikistan police, they would claim to find problems with the documents in order to ask for a bribe. This landlord would not be able to provide the registration stamp, and I had to leave the hotel within the hour without a place to go.

I was panicked and upset, being in this unfamiliar country with nowhere to sleep for the night. I didn't know many people except my new friend from the hotel, so nervously I found him to ask for assistance. It's hard to ask for help, especially in a new place where you don't have deep connections or long-time friends. I felt vulnerable and small. But the man was very kind and sympathetic to my problem. This washed over me warmly, and I felt some relief and hope. He called a few rental agencies and arranged for us to visit rental apartments the same day. This bighearted man then came with me to each one and even helped me carry my baggage on our visits. It took us six hours to visit suitable places while trying hard to find a landlord that could handle the foreigner registrations at the administration office. Many landlords in Tashkent at that time were not willing to do registrations because they would have to declare their property to the government, and that required them to have proper documentation. This was no easy search, especially under the time crunch I was in, but the man stayed by my side, dragging suitcases with me and making calls. Hours had passed. We were tired, sweaty, and feeling a bit defeated as we arrived at the last place on the list.

I was very apprehensive at this point, getting late in the day and still having nowhere to sleep. But this kind man assured me that if this all fell through, I could stay with him and his family.

That was an enormous relief for me. I was deeply grateful for the generosity of my new friend. The feeling was like a ball of light warming my body that someone I had met only days ago was here with me and helping me all day, and willing to take me, a relative stranger, into his own home. There was no financial incentive for him, but just a friendly gesture of incredible kindness and hospitality.

I was amazed at how some people would disrupt their schedules and lives to help others in need.

Eventually, the last place proved a good fit, and I was able to stay there. That experience taught me that you should always see the good in people like my newfound friend did in me. Being on the receiving end of this kindness, I know just how important and life-changing it can be. It does not take much for us to help each other, and I will forever be grateful to this man in Tashkent not only for his help but for showing me this beautiful lesson.

Ghana International Marathon

Sports play a vital role in the development of youth. Sporting competitions give kids a sense of achievement and the capability to analyze their weaknesses in order to conquer them. In doing so, sports provide a dress rehearsal for life's challenges, teaching children to battle against adversity and to accept losses with dignity.

Being an avid long-distance runner for most of my life, I remained rather energetic and had a persistent hunger for adventure. So, I registered for the 2012 Ghana International Marathon within a month of arriving in the country. The marathon was scheduled to be held in the capital city, Accra, and I had two weeks from the time I registered until the event to prepare. I had created a daily regimen that I followed in preparation for the run.

I was already running every day, so training in and of itself wasn't much of an issue for me. The challenge was going to be how I would adapt to the local heat, which threatened to turn my average workouts into unwanted sauna visits — I sweated buckets and had to drink more water than ever before. Nevertheless, I trained every evening in my village of Walewale while loading up on carbohydrates and hydrating as much as I physically could.

Two days before the marathon, I chose to travel out to the capital city. I left on the evening bus, expecting to get some shuteye. Then, after a tiring yet sleepless ten-hour journey in which a continuous and earsplitting Nigerian movie played right above my seat, I reached Accra. The city looked big and beautiful that morning as we pulled into it at around 7 AM: it was host to refined buildings that were many stories high, with plentiful green spaces and bustling roadways.

It was Saturday, and I still had a full day until the race, so I made my way to a colleague's residence in the center of Accra. I took a quick nap at his place. When I woke up, my usual curiosity bombarded me: I wanted to go sightseeing. I vowed that I would not overdo it, that I would conserve my energy for the grueling marathon the next day.

I knew a little about the city and found a tro tro, a Ghanaian van which would take me to the popular Accra Mall. There were only four of us at first, including the driver. I took the front seat, excited to see more of the city while also relaxing. In Ghana, drivers always ensure that the vans are at full capacity before they depart, so we waited. I breathed slowly and deeply, closing my eyes as the van gradually filled.

The sun was ascending higher in the sky, and, even in the shade, we were all crammed together and warm. The man next to me kept moving as I tried to rest, nudging and bumping me as even more people piled in. But I kept my eyes shut and ignored him, and I made a true and earnest effort at ignoring the stifling heat.

On top of these vans, sometimes goats are tied to the roof, an economical way to transfer them from one place to another. I could hear the gentle bleats from above; I smiled as I dozed off.

When the van finally took off, I could hear a constant drip, like what you might get from a leaky faucet. I wanted to assume a multitude of things. Perhaps it had started to rain (not likely). *Were there leaky pipes on van roofs in Ghana?*

I knew there were not. *Did I imagine it?* (I hoped that I had).

When I did open my eyes, fearing the worst, I could clearly see that it was goat urine tumbling down from above. I felt disgusted, but by now, after traveling for a few years, my patience level had become much higher. I looked around the cramped van and could see the drips falling only on top of me from a hole in the ceiling that was right above me. Sometimes, you just have to accept what life throws at you and carry on, even if life decides to throw pungent goat fluids your way while you're sweating from extreme heat.

As I got comfortable again, ignoring the occasional drip, I saw the passenger next to me open a large newspaper and flatten it down on his lap. In fact, when completely unfolded, it splayed across the two of us. I shrugged and let out a quiet sigh. If I could deal with the goats, I could deal with this and, since the newspaper wasn't really touching me, I decided to shut my eyes again until we reached our destination.

A moment later, just as dreams were coming to me, I felt something strange near my pocket and was jolted awake. I swatted whatever insect was there and felt proud that I had dealt with at least one of my problems. The insect must have heeded my warning, for it never tickled me again.

Soon, the person next to me got out of the vehicle, and I had more room to spread out. You don't really appreciate what you have until it has been taken away, and this newfound space and freedom, though still small, felt a lot better. I could even wiggle my feet and give my arms a tiny stretch — it was magic!

When my destination arrived, I got off and reached for my phone, wanting to call my friend to let him know about the goat pee.

My heart leaped into my mouth. My phone was gone.

I slapped my forehead, embarrassed by my own foolishness. I knew exactly what had happened. They were a two-person team, the man with the newspaper and the one behind me. It struck me now that it was so obvious. They had shepherded me into the cramped seat — I had been more easily led than the goats — and had disguised their scheme with a simple newspaper. Looking back, I couldn't even remember what the man looked like who had been sitting behind me, nor could I recall when he had left the van. I had felt him, thinking in my naivety that his hand was a mere insect.

The phone was new, which made me more furious, not because of its price and that I had only just gotten it, but by how easily I was fooled into losing it. I used to consider myself highly aware of whatever was going on around me, and this incident proved me wrong. The sun, as if in on their scheme, beat down on me with even more ferocity as I tried to think about what I should do.

Aggravated and disappointed, I canceled my sightseeing and went back to my colleague's place. I just couldn't stomach it anymore. I was so upset that I also forgot to eat my lunch and hydrate properly for the next day. After a light dinner of pasta that I forced myself to eat, I had my colleague arrange a taxi for 5 AM the following day, to get me to the starting line well before the 7 AM start. Still stressed, I didn't fall asleep until 11 PM that night.

Five and a half hours later, I woke up with bloodshot eyes, got dressed, and waited for the taxi. When he didn't show at 5 AM sharp, I called the driver. From the tone of his voice, I could tell that my call had just woken him up. He insisted that he would pick me up in ten minutes. I begrudgingly waited, then felt that I had been duped a second time when he never came. When I tried to call him back, I found that he had shut off his phone.

Thus, I learned another lesson about not just Ghanaian societal customs but also human mentality. People will often tell you what you want to hear, avoiding confrontation rather than being bluntly honest, as they perceive that honesty will disappoint you. Well, even more so for me, two hours before the marathon that I had signed up for and practiced weeks for in anticipation of.

In order to subdue my anger, I took action: I went out searching for a taxi by myself. It was about twenty minutes after five, and I was walking alone in the middle of Accra in the pitch-black night, the sun only a faint notion on the horizon. I somehow found a driver who was willing to take me to the marathon venue for a reasonable fare. We got there within a half-hour. From that taxi experience, I learned to always have a plan B, and perhaps a plan C, just in case.

At the venue, I saw a load of international athletes from all over the African continent. The best long-distance runners come from Eastern Africa, and I saw several Ethiopians and Kenyans warming up, which made me a little more nervous than I already was. I wanted to give my utmost, which is always the fleeting thought in every runner's mind at the start of a race. I made sure my bib was attached to my shirt so I wouldn't have to fix myself up mid-run, and after a moment of self-motivational talk, I felt prepared for my first competition in Africa.

My mind went back to the hell of the last twenty-four hours as I stretched: the ten-hour bus journey, the dripping that I had tried hard to forget and was sure could be smelled by everyone around me, the stress of losing my phone, a short and troubled sleep, and not enough water to drink or carbs to eat. I didn't have much time to dwell on my sorry state before we were off at the pistol smoke.

The first 20km went reasonably decent — I was well below 90 minutes in. I soon fell into a confident stride. I had made sure to hydrate myself at both the 10km and 20km rest stops. I didn't realize that the sound ringing in my ears was a car horn at first — it was only when I turned my head and almost had a heart attack that I realized we were sharing the road with multiple cars. I found out later that the streets were not closed to traffic while the marathon was being held, and we determined runners just had to accept this fact and keep going amidst the constant honking, exhaust fumes, and mild risk of death. As if imbued by the scene, some street dogs joined in on the commotion, and you were often left with the choice of avoiding either the large lumps of metal on wheels or the snapping white teeth of ravenous hounds. It was all so different from running in Sydney or New York marathons.

I told myself to block out every distraction and keep going.

At about the 30km mark, I really started feeling the heat. Thankfully, I could see a rest stop up ahead. The three people staffing it must have been feeling the heat, too, and seems to have forgotten about the plight of the marathon runners. They had drained most of the drinks themselves. When I got there, there was nothing left. I was outraged — *Are they out of their minds? Do they want to kill us?* — but I resisted the temptation to argue. I didn't want to lose time or waste energy, so I wiped at my sweaty forehead and ran.

Luckily, the universe must have taken pity and me and the runners behind me: a girl running next to me passed me some token, and I purchased a bottle of water from one of the street vendors.

I had just passed the 35km mark, weaving through the heavy traffic as the heat of the day agonizingly accrued, when I saw the athlete in front of me getting into a car. He beckoned me over, inviting me to get in. He promised that the driver would drop us close to the finish line. With a small wave and a shake of my head, I turned down his offer.

If I cheated now, after all of this hard work, I would feel immensely guilty towards the other competitors and let down by myself. I hadn't taken a ten-hour journey from Walewale only to give up so easily. Farther ahead, I saw another athlete on the back of a bike. Some of them openly and remorselessly cheated.

I put everything out of my head and ran. Then, it came into view. What a glorious sight the finish line of a marathon is — an oasis in a desert. I had been running without water for the last 10km or so in the scorching heat of Accra with heavy traffic and barking dogs all around me. I started to sprint towards the finish line when another man fell into step beside me. I looked over at him. He had no bib. Nor had I seen him at the start of the race. He kept running without giving me much more than a glance, so I ignored him.

I reached the finish line. My time was just under four hours. That was much slower than my target time, but I was proud of myself: I had completed the 43km under terrible conditions, but I had done so honestly. Also, I had been in the country for less than a month. The landscape, the environment, was all still unfamiliar to me. Under the circumstances, I had done well, and the grin on my face told that to everyone.

As I walked around after crossing the finish line, I saw the cheating athletes who had taken a taxi and bike. They were proudly receiving their medals. The race authority lacked any chips or cameras to keep track of the athletes, so there was no way to detect who had cheated. I refused to let this rile me. I felt satisfied to have finished my first marathon on the African continent under the harshest conditions that I had ever faced, and I would always feel pride in that race going forward. I ran many races before then and would end up running many more later, but none could compare to the Ghana International marathon of 2012. Even the 2013 Stockholm International Ultramarathon felt incomparable to this one.

The after-race refreshments were to be served in a box after your bib was checked to ensure you were a part of the race. Unfortunately, the massage booth for athletes was full of Ghanaian Government officials and other people. Some had not run the race but were nonetheless enjoying free rubdowns. I felt sorry for the actual athletes.

The winners were from Kenya and had finished the race at least an hour before me. The first three positions received their medals and prize money from the Minister of Sports Authority of Ghana. I knew they had worked hard to race in such conditions in order to finish so quickly. Then I realized how much frustration they must have gone through to maintain their tranquility and perform at that incredible level.

And so, with this experience tucked nicely under my belt, it was no surprise to me that these athletes excel whenever they compete in North America and Europe. Having to work and train so hard in the severe African conditions with limited resources, they would have to develop astounding resilience and courage. I developed enormous respect for those honest African athletes after running this race. And I still look back on it now, feeling grateful that I was able to compete with many impressive individuals.

Fig. 39 Goats on top of the local buses- Ghana

Fig. 40 2013 Ghana International Marathon Finish line

Chapter 13.

Reintegration and Realization

Stationed in a rural area of Afghanistan, I was fortunate enough to be a part of a more authentic community than I probably would have ever seen in an urban setting. Being far removed from the majority of the politics and religious turbulence of more populace places showed me a great deal about the rich Afghan culture. It is in stark contrast to what I had seen on the news and what most people think of when they talk about the nation. Similarly, living in rural Ghana gave me a profound understanding of social norms in African countries within the region – I cannot say that it is the norm across the entire continent because Africa as a continent is so large with diverse heritage.

It has further inspired my interest, and I learned that to really experience the true culture of the country, you have to spend time in the rural areas where people still have a lot of their old customs and culture intact. You need to visit regions that are not heavily influenced by the foreign elements present in capital cities where globalization has influenced them to be more like other cities around the world. An international employee who lives in a capital city is generally in a bubble of comfort and does not always get such an in-depth exposure to the difficulties faced by the natives in rural areas.

A big lesson I learned from all the global living and development missions was to never look down on any culture, especially not knowing the history behind it. Before I learned this lesson, I took a more judgmental approach to the cultures of the people in Ghana, Côte d'Ivoire, and Afghanistan, but every day in these countries made me realize that we are humans with similar emotions. The similarities I have with the people in these places are just as great as with my neighbors at home, and my neighbors at home can have a very different outlook than me. Where we live colors certain aspects of our lives, but we are all still human, making us much more similar than dissimilar, regardless of location. One cannot generalize about a certain culture or a religion.

Culture originates from various historical, religious, and political experiences that occur within a region. Within that context, people behave in a certain way based on what they have faced in their lives. For instance, in some African countries lining up for services is simply not part of their culture; in fact, in some parts of Europe, lines are also not very common.

Many people rush toward the bus, leaving women and children unable to get a seat on public transport. This is mainly because there might not be another bus for a long time. The shortage of resources makes people act in a certain way, whether in Africa, Europe, or southeastern Asia. COVID-19 even highlighted that this is a natural reaction regardless of location; consider how the shortage of certain necessities instigated near panic in the United States, a place that is famous for people queuing up for the things they want. It is more a matter of things being so readily available that lines are more common, but at our core, we will still react based on instinct.

Unfortunately, this type of similarity between nations does go the other way as well. Politics can be misused anywhere in the world, and I saw first-hand how some Afghan politicians see their election as an opportunity to make as much money, even if it demonstrates their own corruption. These politicians know that once they are no longer in power, they will be able to have a very modest lifestyle — helping them to withstand periods of severe shortages.

I saw up close how uneven the world is, that it really does matter where you are born, who your parents are, and your race and ethnicity as to what you will have in life. If you hail from less-fortunate backgrounds, such as a minority group in a war-torn area or a population from a developing country, you begin life at a disadvantage, and you have to work incredibly hard just to reach the starting point of people born in developed nations. Your nationality is of great importance, even though we all should be considered equal. If you are a woman in a conflict zone or a developing nation, life can be much more challenging than that of your male counterparts, and you live under the daily fear of many different types of violence.

My adjustment from developing to the developed country was difficult not only because of the material differences but in the attitudes of the people. In Africa, everyone I met was very friendly and approachable. Without mobile phones and other technology, they have a much stronger human connection with one another. I found that I could speak to anyone on the streets of the villages where I stayed, and I soon became very popular because I was willing to engage and talk with the people.

I never hesitated to call a colleague or a local friend at any time of the day or night if I needed support or assistance. Despite high poverty levels, some people in the open market would also give me free food, such as degue yogurt sachets, as a kind gesture. Many invited me to their place for meals. I never felt threatened by people in any way; I could travel alone anywhere in Ghana on my motorbike without fear.

In Côte d'Ivoire, I lived with a host family in Abidjan who made me feel like part of the family. The house was very modest, with two rooms, and I shared a room with my host brother. In an African context, an elderly woman is greeted as "mama" or "sister," and elderly men as "sir," "brother," or "papa." The cumulative effect was warm and inviting, like I was as much a part of the family and the community. My host brother in Côte d'Ivoire was about my age, and he managed to quickly help me feel acclimated to my home while I was an intern.

When I first entered the house, I looked around and wondered where my room was. With a smile on his face, my host brother showed me the room and bed that we would share. I gulped a bit but composed myself, not wanting to appear rude. Of course, where I am from, this is not considered normal; we would not offer to share a bed with someone whom we were hosting.

"Umm … Together?" I asked apprehensively.

"Of course," he responded, still smiling. Clearly, he did not see the problem, and I was not able to express my own culture's view on this. This wasn't my country, so I would have to get used to the new norms. This was just the first of many.

I wondered where the misunderstanding happened. After all, I had never met him before, and we had only exchanged emails. Then, before I could open my mouth and risk offending my host, I thought about it more. He was treating me like his own brother, and sharing a bed was his way of making me feel like a part of his family. He even offered that he would sleep on the floor in case I was uncomfortable. The host sisters, mother, and father also treated me like their own family. We ate meals together from a big bowl, with all of us surrounding it. I felt like so much more than a guest; I don't remember any time where I felt like a stranger in their home. For as long as I was with them, I was a member of the family.

They also taught me life skills, including how to do laundry by hand, kill a chicken (even though I'm a vegetarian), make the best use of water (shower in a bucket and use that bucket to flush the toilet.), fix motorbikes, avoid encouraging dangerous animals near the house, stand up for myself, and not hesitate to speak loudly in the face of a threat. Above all, they taught me the importance of human connection over a remote connection.

It was quite an emotional scene when I said farewell at the end of my missions. They taught me how vast and diverse this world is, how different our norms are. I could not have so easily believed just how common it is to find things that are acceptable in certain cultures that are absolutely taboo in others. We are all people of different religions, ethnicities, and backgrounds but connected through our shared humanity. Even though I was excited to experience the next stage in life, I was sad to leave people behind—especially those still struggling to survive with few resources and live under the constant threat of terrorism.

Although it was just a two- or three-hour flight, the contrast is striking between the rural, underprivileged areas of the world and places like Europe or North America. I have to admit it was difficult for me to adapt to my old norm after I returned, especially when I came directly from a part of the world suffering because of armed conflict.

After I finished my development mission in Walewale, Ghana, I traveled to Sweden to relax and compete in an ultramarathon. From the moment I stepped off the plane in Stockholm, everything seemed different and intimidating. I lived in a rural African village for only a year, but being suddenly exposed to Stockholm's lifestyle presented a dizzying contrast to my old life. In Walewale, I had mostly eaten rice, corn, porridge, potatoes, bread, beans, bananas, and chicken for the entire year. These were my only options other than occasional chocolates or coffee at a cafeteria in Accra or Bolgatanga. Life was mostly the same every day, with fewer opportunities for recreation. Yet life was enriching because I got daily doses of culture by the daily observations of the people and the intriguing lives that they lived.

Scarcity of clean water was always a big issue back in Walewale. In fact, taps were often locked up. There were no microwaves; some of the people I met didn't even know what a microwave was. Everything was heated on stoves, which may have been healthier but was also time-consuming. Back in Walewale, the limited groceries I bought were from a very small open market that sold few vegetables since not many varieties are grown in the region. I used to also go to a very small shop that sold drinkable water packets, sometimes biscuits and little candies. During my first day in Stockholm, I eagerly visited a supermarket, looked around, and could not believe what I saw. I was absolutely fascinated by the variety of bread, soda, water bottles, and snacks.

In the developed world, we are accustomed to seeing so much abundance that we fail to appreciate just how uncommon that is, not only compared to any other point in history but still today. Far more places do not have this kind of luxury like we do. The foods we are used to every day, like coffee, has long been an integral part of the morning routine for millions of people in the West, along with the ability to regulate temperatures in our houses, use of microwaves, ovens, and other kitchen appliances that help us reduce cooking time drastically. After a year of washing laundry by hand, I was amazed at how easy it was to throw all my clothes in a washing machine. All of these things have become integral parts of our lives and, so without them, we feel incomplete.

In Saharan Africa, people need to travel vast distances just to find enough water to survive, while in the West, clean, temperature-regulated freshwater flows from taps. It sometimes hurt to see wasted in excessively long showers. It is worse when we show just how much we take it for granted by dumping water on our heads in "bucket challenges". The contrast was difficult for me, and I realized it was more than just available products.

In Walewale, Ghana, I got accustomed to being accepted everywhere and hearing the welcoming phrase "ah-lah-fee-ya beh-nee," wishing me good health in the local language of Mampruli. I could talk to anyone on the street and nobody felt threatened. In Stockholm, people on the streets kept their distance from me, and as often as not, avoided making eye contact – a sign that you are in a city. If I'd ask directions from strangers, sometimes they would simply walk away. I remember being excited to be sitting in a cafe for the first time in a long time until I noticed an old lady with a purse that stood between her leg and me. The moment she saw me, her mouth turned down in a frown, and, in a flash of fear, she grabbed the purse and placed it next to her other leg, right next to a Caucasian Swedish man. It was a shocking reaction because back in an African village, no one considered me a threat in any way. But in Stockholm, I felt the subtle signs of unconscious racism toward anyone who didn't look Scandinavian.

Similarly, being out on the streets in Afghanistan taught me many unique and unexpected lessons. Even though I had read a lot about the country before arriving, I was not entirely prepared for the culture shock. In fact, my time in Africa was spent in relative comfort compared to my experience in Afghanistan.

After decades of war and drug abuse, an overwhelming number of people were physically and mentally disabled. Walking down the street, I got used to seeing people who are missing a limb or two, people who clearly exhibited mental illness as they relived battles in their minds, muttering to themselves as they passed or sat off to the sides of where people were walking. To its various invaders, Afghanistan was ground for experimentation with ideology, government, and weapons. None of those invaders cared about the long-term damage they enacted against the people who lived in the country.

During my time there, I learned how to live in a very conservative Islamic environment, where you were not allowed to wear shorts in public, and shaving your beard after it reaches a certain length could get you into trouble. Talking to or eating with female colleagues in public was culturally uncommon and was viewed with suspicion. In fact, it could get the woman into major trouble. I learned how it is tough for people of other sexual orientations to be in Afghanistan, forced to hide who they are. For a man belonging to a lower income group, even getting married was challenging because of the high cost of buying a bride from her family. Polygamy only works for men with higher incomes or wealth and leaves a high proportion of single men to women.

Similarly, people in religious minorities have to make sure that they don't display their faith in public. When I would attend public events like sports or music, I'd look around and notice that women were absent. These events were meant exclusively for men. For musicians or athletes, they would have to be very brave and endure harassment and death threats to follow their dreams. For women in Afghanistan, sexual harassment from men, even men in government offices and public institutions, is not an uncommon occurrence.

Also, I discovered you should never openly discuss taboo subjects like HIV, bacha bazi (sexual abuse of boys by older men), or any social or health issues that revolve around sex. These problems do exist in Afghanistan, but people do not want to acknowledge those issues, opting instead to ignore them. Before judging them, it is important to remember that there are issues that only recently have started being addressed in the West; the rest of the world is just as guilty of ignoring the problem in the name of feeling like they are not common problems.

Finally, keeping a low profile in public is very important, and curfew should be strictly followed. People were tired of decades of war and had completely lost their trust in foreign powers. Many religious leaders and politicians lead a very hypocritical life and do not want any change that would jeopardize their positions of power and influence.

This bothered me the most as I looked around at the wonderful sites in Afghanistan, mainly potential tourist sites the country has failed to develop. Old forts, temples, and monuments all demonstrate the culture of the country. If they maintained these old heritage structures, then there could be a massive increase in tourism, bringing money into the country that would help to better the lives of the people. For instance, Wakhan region is both moderately inhabited and has breathtaking views, so if it were developed, Wakhan could possibly bring in a lot of tourism revenue. Instead, more value is placed on developing shopping malls and other more generic structures rather than spending the funds on maintaining and respecting their cultural heritage.

Despite these problems, I learned that people who live in areas of conflict could be incredibly resilient in ways where people in developed nations would have trouble. People realize that even if life does not change, and the war may not be over soon, they still have lives to live and ways to find enjoyment. I saw some people were comparatively happier, even without the material comforts and safety that we have. One big lesson I learned from the Afghan people was that you don't need to be wealthy to be hospitable and welcoming. Your hospitality toward guests is a state of mind and has nothing to do with how much money you have.

In the West, our lives are easier and more comfortable than those in developing nations, but I wouldn't say we are happier. Experiencing rural African and Afghan life was like a trip through a time machine. Even though we have modern comforts, somehow, our human connections have suffered. People rely a lot more on their financial resources and technology to make them feel fulfilled. Though it's good to always be financially responsible and ambitious, it should not come at the cost of making others unhappy, and it should not be so unimaginably harmful to our environment. When you help others and make their lives better, you truly experience a sense of accomplishment and triumph.

With international living, one realizes that different regions have their own ideas about what beauty standards and bases for physical attractiveness are. This phenomenon again is influenced by the local media that will often depict a certain race, skin tone or physical features to be more appealing in a certain country, but it might be very different in other countries. For instance, in Afghanistan a man's beard demands respect, it is considered an attractive feature and is a part of their culture. It is equally considered professional for office settings. Whereas in North America, being clean shaven is the status quo for a professional look.

One of the shocking realizations I made on my return to Canada was that a lot of people were on anxiety and anti-depression medication. I was aware of it on some level before leaving, but it was only upon my return that I realized just how many people are more anxious about their future. They worry more about accumulating resources than ordinary people in less-developed countries. I noticed that people in developed nations are not particularly eager to socialize or communicate, especially with strangers. They are rather fascinated by technology and infrastructure, locking their eyes on a small screen wherever they go instead of seeing the world around them.

Another aspect is the greeting, that is a vital part of courtesy and goodwill in western culture, but people often fail to wait for a response following their greeting. For instance, people often treat the greeting, "How are you doing?" as a rhetorical question.

According to the World Health Organization, richer countries have higher rates of Generalized Anxiety Disorder than their poorer counterparts. Their depression often reflects in their daily activities, lifestyle, and responsibilities. I have begun a hypothesis that happiness has more to do with the state of mind than the materials at one's disposal, something I would never have believed prior to that first trip to Africa. Also, the social lives and communal spirit of the local people may contribute a great deal to their happiness. This is something that the wealthier communities do not have, and it gives credence to the old saying, "Stomach empty, you have one problem and stomach full you have 100 problems."

In developing countries, people are so engaged in hustling most of the day to earn a minimal livelihood for their families; they don't have so much time to be anxious about the future. With the crowded, vibrant streets and family or friends always nearby, there is an easy way to put their worries into perspective.

These are lessons that cannot be learned by watching the evening news or the movies. Sometimes Hollywood and Bollywood portray war in a glamorous or courageous way, omitting real horrors and realities. Even those that show the horrors of war tend to focus on the soldiers, ignoring the civilians, the mothers, and children who are either caught in the cross-fire or are forced to face a much harsher life in the devastation of their homes. Unfortunately, losing a loved one or a limb is also a way of life for many civilians.

While living in war-torn communities, I noticed the western media loves to amplify any disaster that includes foreigners, especially if it was a terrorist attack. If locals were involved, the media is far less likely to cover the tragedy. This is not just because the media has no interest; they are reacting to the lack of interest of those who consume their content – which is us. Such situations prompt me to wonder if a human's life is less valued because they belong to a least-developed nation.

I needed to make many adjustments to my mindset when I returned to Canada from a war zone. In Afghanistan, I would never approach a gathering of people. In the safety of Canada, I was still hesitant and nervous when I saw a lot of people together—especially if I had to be a part of it. For three years of my life in Afghanistan, I had slept with a combat knife next to my bed. It was either to protect myself in case of an abduction attempt or murder by the Taliban during the night or to kill myself since the last thing I ever wanted was to be taken alive by the Taliban.

Even though I had some martial arts training, it was that small combat knife that gave me more psychological support and confidence every night. I would wake up in the middle of the night, quickly arming myself with my knife whenever I heard any loud noises. During the evenings, I was always alert in my room in the compound. I sometimes would wake up with the noises of fighter jets and helicopters. The sound of active fighting in Kabul is similar to what I experienced at the festival Diwali in India, which had firecrackers as a part of the background sounds. When I returned to Canada, it was a relief in a way that I no longer needed to sleep with the comfort of a knife next to me. Still, the sound of loud noises, even in the safety of Canada, would take me back to the sounds of bombing or gunshots in Kabul, and I would break out into a sweat.

It took me a while to adapt and be able to walk outside in the evening, and even more troubling to board public transportation. If someone wearing a big jacket stood very close to me, my heart rate would increase out of fear he could be a suicide bomber. I would try to keep a distance from people wearing bigger outfits or carrying backpacks. A little shake of the ground in my new apartment in Canada, even during sleep, would send me running outside of the apartment, my mind racing back to the memories of the several earthquakes that I had experienced in Afghanistan.

Throughout my time in Afghanistan, I never saw a woman without a hijab, so I'd feel strange when I saw the opposite sex around me without one even when I returned to Canada. I found it hard to comprehend that a girl or a woman would approach me in public to ask me a question about general directions or ask for other kinds of help. I was just not used to any interaction with the opposite sex—especially in public.

Even my regular greetings, asking someone about their well-being, had changed. I would try to ask people about their families, something that ended up being awkward for many westerners as they find someone asking about their family to be overly personal and uncomfortable. I found people to be much less approachable in Canada after my missions abroad, and the people kept to themselves more. Making friends was difficult. To be respected, one must have a lot of commitments, and lead a busy lifestyle. If I initiated a conversation with a stranger in public transport, they would sometimes wordlessly change seats, leaving me wondering just what I said that might have been offensive. In parts of the world, speaking in a different accent can put you an advantage; in North America, I felt the opposite, that it would put you at a disadvantage in some situations.

Even though I lived in the developed world, I knew that it was just a matter of time before I would largely be reacclimated to my previous ways. However, I realized that it must be much harder for refugees and newly arrived immigrants to learn and adapt to the Canadian or American way of life. The media sometimes portray people in African countries as fierce, cruel, and cold. They spread the wrong impression so much that other parts of the world believe in those incredibly narrow and inaccurate portrayals. I must confess that I had swallowed many such notions, and I had my prejudices before living in Afghanistan.

Having had a firsthand experience, I have come to understand that people are not what the coverage paints them to be. We have so much more in common than we realize. We are only differentiated by race, ethnicity, citizenship, religion, and other social factors because we believe that these aspects are essential and define us as different. The media, politics, or fear of the unknown should not shape our impression of other people.

What the media portrays about the everyday lives of regular people in developing countries is not all of the story. It almost seems they do not want some places to develop, hence, they highlight the most basic aspects instead of showing the beauties and cultures for what they are.

The biggest lesson I learned was to critically analyze the images that the media showed, and hold off forming any strong opinion about a place unless you have personally visited it. Also, you have to question whether or not your country is correct. Independent research is essential for getting a more accurate picture of other places because your country may have a reason for their narrative that doesn't align with the full reality. Fortunately, that is something that is much easier to do today as we can visit the narratives from many other nations and start to piece together the reality.

Living in a higher-income country tends to stifle a sense of curiosity about developing nations and those cultures. Many in developed nations think of developing nations as where they were years or decades ago. They believe that these developing nations will end up more like developed nations. They also pity the citizens who apparently, do not have the same rights and comforts as they have. In reality, developing as a replica of the Western countries isn't right for these communities.

Development and modernization philosophies should not have the template of westernization. Cultural heritage including languages, art, and cultural traditions of every country should always be respected, encouraged, and maintained. It is better to recognize that uniqueness and appreciate what makes us different while remembering that ultimately, we are all still humans, whether we are Afghans, Ghanaians, North Americans, or Europeans.

If you treat someone with respect, they will more treat you likewise, even though the gestures differ according to culture. The hospitality I experienced from people around the world was overwhelming and, despite terrorist attacks, makes me still believe in humanity.

I learned that personal intellect and adaptability are crucial weapons for anyone who desires to succeed in a demanding environment. They are essential tools when dealing with new cultures and customs. This is what Charles Darwin meant when he wrote, "It is not the strongest of the species that survive, nor the most intelligent. It is the most adaptable."

My exposure to developing nations and those caught in the midst of conflict made me realize that I am extremely fortunate to experience a different side of the world, be a part of them, and experience their incredible hospitality.

Overall, I could understand the importance of gratitude and the true meaning of this quote from Helen Keller:

"I cried because I had no shoes until I met a man who had no feet."

About the Author

Ankur Mahajan is an author based in Ottawa, Canada. He works for the Government of Canada and has experience with international organizations and NGOs such as the UN, the Canadian University Service Overseas, the Red Cross, the Association Internationale des Étudiants en Sciences Économiques et Commerciales (AIESEC), the Aga Khan Foundation, and Voluntary Service Overseas.

Having lived in 14 countries, he has completed numerous international aid and development missions in Afghanistan, Côte d'Ivoire, China, Uzbekistan, India, and Ghana. He was educated in the USA, UK, France, Canada, India, and Australia, is a certified project manager (PMP), possesses a Master of Science in Financial Economics from Cardiff University (UK) as well as a Master of Education Studies from Memorial University, Canada, and a Bachelor's of Science in Economics and Management from Purdue University (USA).

Owing to his versatile global living and development missions abroad, he has extensive experience in the social and cultural challenges that workers in international development and diplomacy face.

A linguaphile and a cultural tourist. Ankur is an avid long-distance runner, a participant in several marathons in various countries, a basketballer, and an active judo practitioner who has represented Canada internationally.

He is a vegetarian and has varied interests that include yoga, meditation, theatre, and salsa. He also works at a local bakery on Sundays.

Visit him at www.lifebeyondbullets.com